# DANGERS *of* OFFENCE

## LAWRENCE TETTEH

Published by LT Media Ministries
P. O Box AN 16618
Accra - North
www.lawrencetetteh.org
Tel: +44 (0) 207 357 0910
www.miracletouch.org

# DANGERS OF OFFENCE

Copyright 2006 by Lawrence Tetteh
2nd Edition 2007

ISBN 9988-643-71-3

Printed in Ghana by Combert Impressions
Tel. +233-21-240557

*Unless otherwise indicated, all Scripture quotations are from the King James Version of the Bible.*

# CONTENTS

# DEDICATION

*This work is wholly dedicated to*
**Richard Shakarian**
*of Full Gospel Businessmen's Fellowship*
*for carrying on the vision of his father,*
*Demos Shakarian.*

*Also dedicated to the following giants in the Ministry in Ghana:*

Rev. Dr. Samuel Asante-Antwi
Rev. Dr. Sam Prempeh
Rev. Dr. Robert Aboagye-Mensah
Rev. Dr. Frimpong-Manso
Archbishop Justice Akrofi
Peter Cardinal Appiah Turkson
Archbishop Gabriel Palmer-Buckle

*And to my spiritual father and mentor,*
Rev. Francis Akwasi Amoako
(Of Blessed Memory)

# ACKNOWLEDGEMENTS

My special thanks to the Holy Spirit, for inspiring me to write
this book on the "Dangers of Offence."

Dr. Ron Kenoly, Dr. T.L. Osborn, Papa Ayo Oritsejafor and
Pastor Sam Larbie, thanks for your encouragement.

Also to Janet, Olivia, Doreen and Roger for proof-reading the
scripts

Special thanks to my dad and mum, Mr. and Mrs. Tetteh.
Also to my siblings Alex, Prince, Lady Gifty, Pastor Eben,
Victoria, Princess and Grace, for binding the family together.

My warmest appreciation to my wife, Barbara,
for your continuous support through the years.

**God bless you all!**

# INTRODUCTION

*For it is not an enemy who reproaches me; Then I could bear it. Nor is it one who hates me who has exalted himself against me; Then I could hide from him. But it was you, a man my equal, my companion and my acquaintance. We took counsel together, and walked to the house of God in the throng. (Psalm 55:12-14)*

## Background

My initial thoughts for writing on the subject of offence came to me on a flight from France to a country in Central Africa. I was with about fifteen others in the first-class section. We had boarded the plane and prior to take-off, we were being served drinks. A lady asked the flight attendant for orange juice but instead she was served with pineapple juice. This lady on seeing the pineapple juice was so upset that she began to rain insults on the flight attendant and ended up pouring the entire glass of pineapple juice on the attendant's face. The attendant did not get the chance to offer any explanation.

The purser was called and the captain subsequently informed. He, on his part, decided that he would not allow such behaviour and abuse on his flight. Security was called in to offload the lady from the flight. By this time, having grasped the implications of her excesses, the lady was crying and apologetic but she was still taken off the flight. She made her undignified exit, totally disgraced and embarrassed. Her behaviour had even caused the flight to be delayed.

As we flew, I reflected on the incident and her disgraceful behaviour and thought of the possible repercussions on her position in the company she represented; her career, both short and long term and a whole range of possible outcomes. She may have lost so much by that one rash action. I looked at it as the devil having trapped her and she having been caught totally off-guard. I realised how important it was to guard against being caught out by the devil through reacting in offence.

**What Is an Offence?**

Offence in the simplest terms is when a person becomes angry or has hurt feelings. When we are offended, we experience a bewildering array of emotions ranging from physical pain, hurt feelings, confusion, rejection, shock, amazement etc. We are left feeling wounded and bitter. Our instinct is not to forgive whoever hurt us. Our natural human instinct takes over and because we do not want to be so vulnerable as to be hurt again, we begin to build a protective wall around our hearts. We become wary of those who are close to us. This is because they are most likely to hurt us, simply because of our close relationship with them. If something goes wrong with that relationship, we burn up so much energy in withholding access to our hearts that we become hardened and insensitive. This attitude becomes a stumbling block leading to mistrust, torment of our minds and the distortion of our perceptions.

Offence is at the root of most problems. It could be caused by words, either uttered or written; by looks, facial expressions, tone of voice, gesture or body language. Something which may offend one person may not offend another. Whereas a simple, harmless passing comment intended to be humorous can cause offence to one person, another person may laugh it off and move on. Whether a person takes offence at something or not depends on their peculiar perception of the matter and their mood at the time.

Offence can cause you to walk in denial, and keep up a false impression, whilst you are full of anger, malice, hatred etc. The person harbouring offence or negative emotions inside them is as guilty as the one who is open about his emotions. You can create an impression of being super-spiritual, suppress your anger, and destroy yourself.

*Are you offended?*
*Have people caused you grief?*
*How would Jesus react to this?*
*Friends are fighting friends*
*Pastors are fighting pastors*
*Presidents are fighting presidents*
*Politicians are fighting politicians*
*Everybody is defending a cause.*
*What would you do?*
*If Jesus had been in your shoes,*
*Would He have run off to spread the evil report?*

Offence works both ways. We are human, and just as we become offended, so also do we offend. If we try to remember this, it will be easier not to take offence. No one is immune to offence and it comes from various sources. Some people are offended by society; they are angry and blame society for all their woes. Some are even angry with God, whom they blame for the pressures and challenges of life. In the opinion of some others, religion is to blame for wars, disunity and all other problems in the world. The Gospel is seen as an offence to those who are perishing, so they choose to persecute those who carry it. Even the name "Jesus" is offensive to some people. The religious establishment in Christ's day took offence at His message, opposed Him and eventually orchestrated His crucifixion.

It is not wise to take to heart everything you hear about yourself. This is because we are all guilty of offending someone. For example, you could say something unkind about someone and it is likely that someone else will say something uncomplimentary about you too. The Bible says in Ecclesiastics 7:21-22, "*Also do not take to heart everything people say, lest you hear your servant cursing you. For many times, also, your own heart has known that even you have cursed others.*"

It is my prayer that you do not allow yourself to be ensnared by the enemy, and that by the time you finish reading this book, you will say to yourself, "Offence is not my destiny. I am settling for nothing but the best. I shall not accept anything less." Remember what Jesus said, "The devil comes to kill, to steal and to destroy. But I have come that ye may have life and have it more abundantly." John 10:10. God Bless You.

Chapter

# 1

# WHAT DOES OFFENCE DO?

In order to fully understand the damaging impact of offence, it is important to observe the ways in which it affects us. Offence steals our joy. It is destructive to our lives and can kill if we allow it. It affects us individually as well as our relationship with God and others. It is like a cancer that eats us up, and like a virus that spreads and infects others around us. Offence can affect your spiritual growth as a Christian and unsettle both your mind and body. It is the root of all bitterness and can lead to tension, conflict, misbehaviour and the weakening of our faith.

Through offence, many have been distracted or diverted from their destiny; they have lost their focus, position, status and even their anointing. Offence can change your nature or character, influence your relationships, lead you into disgrace or even turn you into a criminal. It can drag you into litigation with adverse financial consequences and implications. Offence can make you arrogant, cause you to speak or act contrary to your intellectual capability. It can make you lose authority and make you forget what God has promised you. It can also cause you to lose what you have laboured for.

Offence can affect your prayer life, destroy your home, take away your privileges, lead you to create alliances with 'wrong' people and cause havoc in relationships with relatives, friends, church members, work colleagues, business partners and the community in which we live and work. It also brings about disunity and wrecks fellowship between believers. It is our reactions that create the problems associated with offence.

> *Offences are the devises of the enemy to obstruct you from reaching your goal.*

Offence is nothing new for it has been part of human existence as far back as creation. Throughout the Bible, there are examples of people who took offence and behaved irrationally to their own detriment, sometimes with tragic consequences. Others faded out and were not heard of thereafter in the Bible even though they could have achieved more for God instead of disappearing into oblivion.

David's eldest brother, Eliab, was one such person. In 1 Samuel 17:23-28 Eliab was serving in King Saul's army. David at the time was assigned to look after their father's sheep. Upon arrival at the battlefield to deliver food to him and his two other brothers from their father, David did not immediately go back to tend the sheep. His father wanted feedback about the battle, so he stayed around and wanted to know more about what was going on and also about Goliath's challenge. Eliab took offence at his younger brother and angrily rebuked him. He used his position as a senior brother to openly reprimand David before the people. In verse 28 he said, *"Why camest thou down hither? And with whom hast thou left those few sheep in the wilderness? I know thy pride, and the naughtiness of thine heart; for thou art come down that thou mightest see the battle."*

David then answered back in verse 29 saying, *"What have I done now? Is there not a cause?"* The controversy ended because David ignored him and went ahead to challenge and defeat Goliath. God used David on that day to defeat the fearsome Philistine army. As a result, Eliab's authority over David was completely undermined; firstly because David had to answer back in front of the people, and secondly because subsequent actions vindicated his refusal to leave as Eliab had directed. Having served in the army, and with his battle experience, Eliab could easily have been named as one of the mighty men of David's army in later life. However, Eliab was never heard of again or mentioned in the Bible.

The origin of domestic violence can be traced to the very first two brothers in the Bible, namely Cain and Abel. Cain took offence at his brother Abel and was jealous because Abel's offering was accepted by God while his was rejected. His jealousy was carried beyond the limit and he rose up in rage and murdered his brother, Abel. Genesis 4:1-16 records that, as a result, God cursed Cain and he became an outcast living in exile.

In Genesis 37, Joseph's brothers took offence because he was their father's favourite son. He further provoked them when he revealed his dreams of greatness to them, so they sold him into slavery. Jealousy and hatred caused them to carry out such an evil deed by selling their brother off and convincing their father that he had been killed. Similarly, in Judges 11, Jephthah's half-brothers threw him out of the house, due to hatred because his mother's actions as a prostitute were offensive to them.

In I Samuel 25, David took offence because Abigail's husband, Nabal, had sent a rude message back to him when he asked for some food to feed David's men in their camp. David had protected Nabal's sheep in the past and felt that the latter owed him a favour. Instead, the drunken Nabal pretended not to remember David and rather insulted him as a vagabond. The threat from David to kill Nabal and all his men in retaliation terrified him so much that he eventually suffered a heart attack and died.

John the Baptist went ahead of Jesus as the forerunner. They were cousins, and John knew perfectly well that Jesus was the Messiah and he had openly admitted this in his messages. He even said before baptising Jesus, in Matthew 3:11, that he was unworthy to untie or carry Jesus' sandals. However, when he was cast into prison, in Matthew 11:1-3, he sent his followers to go and ask Jesus if he was the Messiah or they should wait for another. Why? He heard about all the things Jesus was doing, and perhaps expected Jesus to do something about his imprisonment. John must have been offended or felt dispirited, disappointed or betrayed because he did not receive a visit from Christ.

Jesus Christ Himself was offended a number of times by His brothers, mother, sisters, disciples and the religious establishment of His day, but He did not allow the offence to distract Him from his purpose on earth. We see in Mark 6:1-5 that the one who was hailed as the Messiah, King of the Jews, Rabbi,

Son of God, Teacher, Master and other such titles by many, was disrespected and rejected when He went to Nazareth, His hometown. So great was the resentment that he could not perform any miracles there.

The dangers of offence are evident around us all the time. Offence cuts across all spectrums of society; irrespective of class, race, colour or sex. It is part of human nature and the instinctive reaction is to hit back at the offender.

Throughout my travels around the world, I have noticed that one of the major things that have kept most believers from effectively impacting society and taking the world for Christ, as we are commissioned to do, is offence. We fight each other all the time, and consequently there is disunity in the body of Christ. We do not relate well and work together to proclaim the Gospel with a united front. We read in Psalm 133 *"Behold how good and how pleasant it is when brothers live together in unity."* Unity brings the favour, glory and blessings of God.

Think about this! How close were you with that brother or sister before you fell out with each other? When you really think about it now, how serious was the offence? Could it not have been settled amicably and the relationship maintained or restored if one or both of you had stopped to reflect instead of reacting as you did? The most important thing to know is that it is the plan of the enemy to stop what God has destined for you. We need to resolve offensive issues in order to maintain peace and unity in our homes, relationships, and in the church. **When you offend somebody, after explaining yourself in all sincerity, just move on.**

The devil attempts to entrap us by using the challenges and problems we face in our daily lives, our relationships and in the course of implementing our plans to achieve his destructive purposes. If we are not smart enough, he succeeds in setting us back. He is so subtle and clever that quite often we do not even realise that it is his influence on our thoughts that cause offence. Once he succeeds in planting these thoughts, they trigger off a chain reaction which could have far-reaching negative consequences and cause disruptions in our lives.

It is my greatest desire that you open your hearts, minds and spirits to receive the insight and understanding that this book can give you. It can help you deal with offence in your own life and defeat the enemy in his ploy to derail and prevent you from fulfilling your God-given purpose in this life. Open your eyes and be alert for the enemy's intention is to make you lose your place in history!

Practical day-to-day issues such as pride, lack of communication, ignorance or lack of understanding easily generate offence. We get offended, basically, when our ego is deflated or our pride is hurt, hence the tendency to behave irrationally. Naaman, the commander of the Syrian army was a great man held in high esteem, a man of valour; but he suffered from leprosy. In the account in 2 Kings 5:1-18, when the Prophet Elisha sent word for him to go and wash seven times in the river Jordan for his healing, he took offence at the advice, because he believed that the waters in Syria were better than the River Jordan. He was enraged, and turned away because of pride. It took the persuasion of a servant, to bring him back to his senses, thus making Naaman receive his healing miracle. Some people allow pride to stop them from responding to altar calls at church, and so they miss out on the work God is waiting to do in their lives. We need to humble ourselves in the sight of God before we can receive breakthroughs and blessings.

Pride is at the root of all sin instigated by Satan. Offence is sin in scriptural terms. Satan took offence at God because of pride. He was in the worship team as a worship leader in heaven, but saw himself as great as God his Creator. He wanted to exalt himself to God's position. God, therefore, drove him and a third of the angels who aligned themselves with him out of Heaven. Satan now roams about in this world like a roaring lion always seeking an opportunity to devour somebody, and to cause havoc by killing, stealing our blessings and destroying our lives.

Goliath the Philistine giant, was full of pride, and was so incensed by the fact that a rustic-looking teenage boy, 16 ½ years old would come to challenge him for a fight. He was 9 feet tall, a trained warrior and the leader of the Philistine army. David had no experience with any weapon of war. He relied only on God's power and his experience gained in protecting the sheep in the bush. The only semblance of a weapon he had was the catapult and stones he wielded as he approached Goliath, who was heavily clad in armour. Goliath was very offended and ridiculed David; but this unsuspecting, boastful giant lost his power and authority, and suffered a very humiliating death. A simple stone that would normally be only suitable for killing birds was used to kill him. This was so disgraceful to a man of his position and rank. This story in 1 Samuel 1:17 confirms how low God can bring us when we become arrogant and boastful and forget that He is the one who gives us any power we may have.

Sometimes you take offence when someone misunderstands you, insults your intelligence or questions your choice or decision. You could be offended when you think somebody is challenging your position at home, work, church or even your authority. Also when someone questions your judgement, disrespects or belittles you, or is arrogant towards you or even when society treats you different from what you think you deserve.

We react to offence according to our level of emotional stability. We all have different personalities and different temperaments. Some people have very sensitive dispositions, and are therefore quick to react when offended. Some are able to control their emotions well, while others internalise their emotions, and pretend that there is no problem and that 'all is well'. Such people often retaliate later and can be very dangerous. Some people are not easily offended, and so may ignore any offence or deal with it lightly and move on. What matters most is how well you are able to deal with the offence. Repressing your anger and allowing it to fester is not the way forward. It is damaging to your faith and health.

**Be Mindful**

Sometimes we allow the enemy to put poisonous thoughts into our minds. It is good to ask ourselves the following questions:
- How do we respond to our mind's promptings?
- What caused us to react the way we did?

- Did we find out if there was truth or falsehood in what we heard or saw?
- Could it just be wrong thoughts because of the sentiments in our hearts, or some past experience?

Wrong thoughts do not only affect your spiritual growth but can generate offence in you and even cause you to kill. What you think of or hear repeatedly registers on your mind and becomes a picture of good or evil that can affect you and cause you to react accordingly. Do you pause, think and see how lovingly or otherwise you respond to your relations, neighbours and to your brothers and sisters in Christ? Do you pause to consider the consequences of your own possibly offensive behaviour?"

We need to reprogramme our minds because it is the wrong perceptions of the mind that mostly cause us to be offended. An innocent look, for example, from somebody can cause you to react offensively, if your mind plays it falsely to you and you misinterpret this look.

This book aims to reveal the dangers of both offending others and becoming offended. It shows some of the causes and effects on our physical lives, businesses, finances, health, emotions, reactions, perceptions, peace of mind and our spiritual lives, to mention just a few. The roots of offence and their reasons are therefore so complex that it is impossible to totally unravel them. In actual fact there is no area in our lives which is not affected when we take offence. As we react to offence, we become diverted or derailed from God's pre-ordained path for us and we fail to fulfil our destiny or potential. We change course, even if it is only slightly, and head in a direction different from what God intended for us. This of course delights the devil whose sole aim is to kill us, steal our joy or virtues, and redirect our focus. He is a subtle, strategic schemer and we have to be very alert, observant and discerning as we walk along the paths of life.

I intend also to show you the way forward to overcoming the feelings of anger, resentment, bitterness, sadness, hurt etc. that are created through offence and how to avoid the devil's trap to draw us into sin, steal from us, change our destinies and lead us into captivity. Many of us Christians are in denial that we are wounded through offence. We have buried our hurts so deeply that we are not even aware that they are still there. We need to ask the Holy Spirit to reveal the true state of our hearts to us. Once we acknowledge what we are harbouring within our hearts, we can begin the corrective action to enable us to deal with its negative effects. We can then seek healing so that our spirits can become unblocked from unforgiving attitudes and bitterness, and we can once more become receptive to the Holy Spirit and to God's plan for us.

Chapter

2

# AN UNFORGIVING SPIRIT

*"If your brother sins against you, rebuke him; and if he repents, forgive him. And if he sins against you seven times in a day, and seven times in a day returns to you, saying, "I repent" you shall forgive him."(Luke 17:3-4)*

## Cancel the Debt They Owe You

An unforgiving spirit is usually the major cause of every problem related to offence. It forms the cornerstone of the building which houses all negative effects of offence. An unforgiving nature creates hurt and a wrong desire for revenge which blocks our spirits whilst we are trying to rationalise our actions and reactions, and the need to justify ourselves. It stems from a lack of genuine love. We read in 1 Corinthians 13: 5 that, *"Love does not insist on its own rights or its own way, for it is not selfseeking: it is not touchy or fretful or resentful; it takes no account of the evil done to it"* (This means that it pays no attention to a suffered wrong).

True forgiveness is one of the most difficult things to give. This is seen in Luke 17:1-4 when Jesus spoke to His disciples. After stressing the fact that offence was inevitable, he urged them to continually forgive those who offend them. The disciples' answer to the Lord was, "Increase our faith." In other words, they found it difficult to forgive continuously by their own strength. They felt that acceptance of that needed a greater level of faith and so they asked Jesus to increase their faith. The disciples had seen many miracles like raising of the dead, healings, walking on water, calming seas etc. without asking for extra faith, but when it came to forgiveness, they asked for an increased faith in order to do what Jesus was commanding them to do. It is therefore not surprising that we find forgiveness so difficult. It is necessary for our own good, both physically and spiritually, to forgive.

In Matthew 18: 21-35, Jesus advises Peter to forgive seventy times seven times. Jesus illustrates an unforgiving attitude here with the parable of the unmerciful servant who had received his master's kindness but could not show same to his fellow servant who owed him much less. Jesus ended the parable by illustrating the end of the unforgiving; "*And in his anger his Lord delivered him to the jailers, till he should pay all his debt. So also my heavenly Father will do to every one of you, if you do not forgive your brother.*"

We suffer mental torture if we do not forgive. It is as if we have been imprisoned in a torture chamber of bitterness and resentment with spears sticking into and cutting up our hearts. That, unfortunately, is the punishment we bring upon ourselves when we refuse to forgive and let go.

Jesus said, in Matthew 5:7, "*Blessed are the merciful for they shall obtain mercy.*" Mercy is forgiveness. Since we all want to receive God's mercy, we must do what it takes and that means we must forgive others.

As Christians we must follow the Master's example by forgiving and praying for the offender. Jesus Himself demonstrated the ultimate example of forgiveness to us by dying on the cross for us. He also showed us the greatest love we could ever know through this. As He hung on the cross in much pain, having taken all the abuse, insults, taunts, name calling, scourging, mockery etc, Jesus asked God the Father to forgive His tormentors. He prayed for them saying, **"Father forgive them, for they know not what they do."( Luke 23: 34).**

Naturally, as human as you are, your feelings would include hurt, anger, outrage and bitterness and you may have a strong desire for revenge. Instinctively, you may cry out to God to strike your offenders with lightening and thunder or curse them and all their future generations with the worst curses imaginable. Jesus however, did not do this and as His true followers, we must also forgive and pray for those who cause us pain. He came down as a normal human being and felt all the emotions that we feel, but the difference is that He handled offence differently. We must follow His example in order to experience true peace, breakthroughs and an abundant flow of anointing.

An unforgiving attitude fosters bitterness and can cause you to be restless and lose sleep. These can with time develop into a stronghold and cause many health problems like insomnia and depression. The consequences of offence are many and varied:

## 1.    Offence Can Make You Seek Revenge

A pastor who feels offended sometimes chooses to curse the person whom he, rightly or wrongly, thinks has caused the offence to him.  Sadly, he uses the Bible to curse and command death over the purported offender, because 'he is an enemy'. Is he pleasing God or the devil? Offence can poison your spirit with hatred. Angry words can reveal what is in your heart. Some people pick quotations out of context to justify their actions and vengeful prayers. God does not answer such prayers.

Perhaps, you have offended somebody and have either not accepted your mistake, or refused to, but you are asking God to kill the one you perceive to be your enemy. He does not die as you expected, so you continue to show hatred and hostility towards him. Are you right? By calling for the death of your enemy, you are denying them the opportunity of repentance or salvation. If you reflect on your motives for revenge, you will realise that they are wrong. God looks at your heart and motives as well as timing and other factors in answering prayers, and very often we, not knowing the bigger picture, choose to question God and His ways. This of course leads only to constant disappointment. Jesus abounds in love and is the giver of life.

John 3:17 tells us, *"For God did not send His Son into the world to condemn the world, but that the world through Him might be saved."* In 2 Peter 3: 9 we read that *"The Lord is... not willing that any should perish but that all should come to repentance."* ˙

Offence can cause you to dwell on your carnal mind to resolve issues and deny yourself the peace of God. Your thoughts are not the thoughts of God, and neither are your ways the same as God's ways. Leave the situation in His hands.

God loves the person who has wounded you, and it is His will for that person not to perish but to come to know Him. The plan and purpose of God for any man is not known until He himself reveals it. *"For it is God who works in you both to will and to do of His good pleasure"* (Philippians 2:13). Jesus commands us to **pray for our enemies and bless rather than curse them.**

An associate minister, who was wrongly accused of embezzling church funds, became so offended that in his anger he plotted to commit arson and burn the church down. There was so much anger and hatred in his heart as well as a yearning for revenge that he was prepared to risk going to prison for his planned act. The said accusation was apparently levelled as a way of destroying his reputation and disgracing him simply because he wanted to leave the church. The whole episode caused a great deal of distress to his family. As a result, his wife left the church in anger. He however changed his mind and braved the storm; he forgave his accusers, and stayed in the church until some time later. Subsequently, he was vindicated and at the appointed time, God promoted him into a different kind of ministry altogether where he is now happily settled. Thank God for His grace.

We live in a world or society where people do what they want, sometimes with little or no regard for those around them. People, for their own selfish motives, do unjust things, are wicked, create offence and cause great hurt or pain to one another. This is why some people go to extremes to settle their own scores. This is, however, contrary to biblical teaching.

## 2.    Offence Can Make You Act Foolishly and Lose Respect

Two feuding charismatic pastors of a particular church in London shamefully engaged in a brawl, which ended up in a 'punch-up' after church one Sunday in front of their church members. They both ended up on the ground. What a disgrace! Unfortunately, the problem that triggered off the offence was still not resolved and could not possibly have been resolved with the fight. The two ministers had fallen prey to the devil's strategy of allowing hatred and anger to be fuelled in each of them to the extent that it had spilled over. They had fallen into the devil's trap to bring them shame, steal their joy and disgrace them openly. Offence can make you behave as foolishly as one who has lost his intellectual ability or common sense. Their immaturity had a negative impact on the church, eventually causing it to split up.

Such disunity, conflict and misbehaviour also block the flow of God's blessings and the Holy Spirit. Power from heaven will not flow down into a church where there is no unity; and there will certainly be no numerical or spiritual growth.

## 3.   Offence can make you commit Murder

A typical example in the Bible was Esau who was deeply offended when his brother Jacob, with the aid of his mother, stole his blessing from their father, Isaac, in Genesis 27. Jacob had to flee into exile to escape the wrath and revenge of Esau. Esau was so offended and hurt that he cried out in pain. He felt cheated out of his blessing and betrayed, so he went out searching for Jacob, intending to take revenge by killing him (v.41). This is real evidence of why offence can be so dangerous. Jacob managed to flee with the connivance of his mother, Rebekah. Esau's anger was his yoke, and it was stirred up when his brother offended him.

Eventually, he managed to do something about this yoke. Many years later, Esau met up with his brother. Jacob offered restitution and there was reconciliation between the two brothers. When you feel cheated and betrayed by a friend or relation, remember that Esau forgave his brother Jacob and their brotherly relationship was restored.

When we are unforgiving, we harbour sin in our hearts, which causes us to sin. Like a growing plant, it has many side shoots. It can cause bitterness and hatred leading to murder.

The Bible tells us in I John 2:9, "*He who says he is in the light, and hates his brother, is in darkness even until now.*" In other words he is deceiving himself that he is in the light. It also says in I John 3:15, "*Whosoever hates his brother is a murderer, and you know that no murderer has eternal life abiding in him.*"

## 4. It Creates Discord in the Home

An unforgiving attitude commonly creates discord in the home. The family is a focus of attack by Satan because it is the major centre of God's blessings for humanity. These are some of the dangerous ways he enters families and tears them apart when offence is not dealt with sensibly:

- Husband and wife fighting, leading to domestic violence, possible injury and criminal prosecution.
- Husbands and wives becoming extremely touchy and argumentative. An unfortunate wrong choice of word by one partner can become an issue blown out of all proportion.
- Children being unhappy at the lack of financial support from parents.

Any of these can cause devastation, heartbreak, pain, betrayal, bitterness and resentment in the hearts of the husband, wife and children and can result in loss of confidence and the destruction of the home.

It leads to distrust and a breakdown of communication in the home. Everything said or done, all actions, expressions and even the way one party regards the other is treated with suspicion and critically observed and examined for ulterior motives. All sorts of interpretations are given to simple issues. Sinister moves are seen where they do not exist and the relationship becomes extremely strained. At the worst, it can lead to a marriage breakdown or divorce with its unpleasant financial, emotional, spiritual effects as well as the adverse impact on the children. Marriage break-up is a breach of covenant with God.

The family unit disintegrates and it affects the children who can become rebellious or introverted because of deep pain, and the feeling that their parents have betrayed them by breaking up. It makes them distrustful of adults and they feel they cannot pour their hearts out to anyone since the adults (parents) they had trusted totally, have let them down. They bottle things up and start misbehaving by rebelling against their parents and society. Sometimes, they end up joining bad company resulting in crime, drugs or prostitution. Worse still, it can cause them to view marriage or relationships with the opposite sex negatively, which is not healthy for their future.

## 5.    It Changes Your Character

The hurt, bitterness, confusion, shock, betrayal, feelings of rejection, devastation, resentment and other conflicting emotions that are set in motion because of offence can cause a person to change from being a happy, cheerful and trusting person to a suspicious, bitter and fearful one. These result in loss of self confidence and can make a person very cautious and defensive in their outlook towards life. It can lead to a person becoming or exhibiting one or some of the following undesirable characters:

a.    *Resentful and Confrontational.* It may be that somebody refused or could not do you a favour so you became offended and confronted or attacked that person. John and his brother James, who were among the twelve disciples of Jesus, were offended because they could not have what they wanted. They were so angry that they wanted Jesus to permit them to take revenge on a Samaritan town for not welcoming them. They asked, in Luke 9:54, "*Lord do you want us to call fire down from heaven to destroy them even as Elijah did?*"  But Jesus turned and rebuked them.  And he said, "*You do not know what kind of spirit you are of, for the Son of Man did not come to destroy men's lives, but to save them.*" Jesus nick-named them thereafter as the "sons of thunder." John later got rid of his fiery temper and went on to become the most loving disciple. His letters are all based on love for one another.

Offence can cause you to be resentful and confrontational. For example, you trusted someone with some delicate personal information and they betrayed your trust. When you hear some damaging gossip regarding your shared confidences, the hurt can cause you to react angrily by attacking the person you believe to be responsible. As you allow more feelings of resentment to settle into your spirit, it takes root, develops into bitterness and eventually changes your nature. You will be harming yourself and could die a slow and foolish death through medical conditions like cancer, high blood pressure etc triggered off by the physical effects of harbouring bitterness in your heart. Is it worth your life or health? Why not release offence from your heart and let go of the matter?

**b. Angry and Bitter (By stealing your joy).** Another case could be where you are going through trials, are discontented or think God is unkind to you and you become angry and begin to doubt him. You become impatient with God because things have delayed and afflictions have overwhelmed you. You become so angry and bitter that it changes your attitude and outlook. This is a sure bait of the devil and if you let the trials etc. change you, you would have fallen into his trap. The bitterness or anger opens you up to more attacks from the enemy.

Remember that when Job was sorely tempted, he refused to fall into the devil's trap and do anything sinful against God even though people around him encouraged him to. In the end, he was victorious. Remember that trials are a time of testing, and are like an examination. We need to pass them. Without going through them we cannot know our level of maturity. We become stronger people for having gone through them. They are the fire that we need to go through, to become pure gold. For this reason, we should thank God for all the trials and challenges we go through because they are preparing us for the great things that God has for us. They are the training ground. If we give up or succumb to the devil, it tells God that we are not ready for promotion yet.

**c. Stubborn and Hard-hearted.** Offence can cause you to

develop a stubborn and impatient heart that prevents you from experiencing the glory of God. You harbour iniquity in your heart. If there is iniquity in your heart, as David said in Psalm 66:18, God will not listen to your prayer. Romans 2:5-6 tells us that, *"In accordance with your hardness and impenitent heart, you are treasuring up for yourself wrath and revelation of the righteous judgement of God. God will render to each one according to his deeds."*

Iniquity stops the joy, blessings and favour of the Lord from flowing through you and to you. The stubbornness and hardness of your heart can become a bondage and stronghold taking control of your life. All these negative things will cause you to become insensitive to human feeling and affect your countenance. It will also bring the righteous judgement of God upon you. Proverbs 15:13 states that *"A merry heart makes a cheerful countenance, but by sorrow of the heart the spirit is broken."*

## 6.    It Distorts Your Perception

In Luke 11:33-36 it says, "When your eyes are sound your whole body is full of light." When you are consumed with negative emotions and an unforgiving spirit because of offence, the light in you becomes darkness and you will not see well. Offence distorts your true perception. You see things from a negative point of view. What is black may seem like red to you. A blessing of God coming your way may be seen as part of an evil plan and viewed with suspicion.

You interpret everything from a negative point of view and lose out on all kinds of blessings. Your perception is distorted because you put on blinkers and do not see positive things approaching. In relationships and everyday life, you always look round for someone to blame whenever things go wrong. You will see nothing good in the one who has offended you even though they may have been your best friend in times past. Even if the person is ready to make amends and comes to you with an olive branch, you refuse it because you are in the chamber of resentment and bitterness and you are unforgiving.

## 7.    It Makes You Judgemental, Condemning and Critical

When you live with offence, your life is characterised by hatred, jealousy and intolerance. It affects your attitude, and you are in danger of standing in judgement. You have no right as a person, to judge others. If you do, you may deny yourself of God's move in your life, and the position you may have been promoted to. It is God who sits on the judgement throne and judges all. No one is without offence. As Christians we should take our example from Jesus. When the woman who was caught in adultery red-handed, was brought before him, Jesus spoke to the accusers and said, he who is without sin let him cast the first stone, and behold all her accusers left her and went away in shame. Jesus said to her, **neither do I condemn you but go and sin no more**.

Luke 6: 37, also tells us to *"Judge not, and you shall not be judged. Condemn not, and you shall not be condemned. Forgive and you will be forgiven."*

## 8.    Refusal to forgive can release God's wrath against you.

Numbers 16: 1-35 tells us about the rebellion of Korah, Dathan, and Abiram. It came about because they took offence at Moses' style of leadership. They complained, criticised and judged him because they thought they should all be in equal leadership. The consequence of their offensive behaviour was that God opened up the earth and it swallowed them and their families alive. The earth closed up on them and they all died. Then, God sent out fire from heaven and burnt alive 250 other people who were their followers.

Has some church member done something you find offensive? Did you become cold towards the person and set about tongue-wagging, insulting and gossiping? Did you pass judgement about them? Romans 2:1 admonishes us that, *"Whoever you are who judge, for in whatever you judge another you condemn yourself, for you who judge practice the same things."*

## 9.    Offence can have Criminal Consequences

Offence can lead you into violence and even possibly, into murder. In 2 Samuel 13, Amnon raped his half-sister Tamar (Absalom's sister). For two years Absalom went about his life as if he had forgiven and forgotten it, but he harboured the offence in him until he invited Amnon to a banquet, took revenge and got him killed at the banquet table. Fearing the king's wrath, Absalom fled and was in exile for three (3) years.

When you continually carry out criminal acts out of revenge, it dulls your conscience and makes you callous. You become insensitive to emotions or to what is right or wrong and you become a ready tool for the devil.

David wrote in Psalm 36:1-4, *"Transgression speaks to the wicked deep in his heart. There is no fear of God before his eyes. For he flatters himself in his own eyes, when he finds out his iniquity and when he hates. The words of his mouth are wickedness and deceit; He has ceased to be wise and to do good. He devises wickedness on his bed; He sets himself in a way that is not good. He does not abhor evil."*

**What Do I Do?**

**a. Pray and ask the Holy Spirit to help you release your hurt.**

You may remember people whom you hold something against as you read this book. Sit quietly and let the Holy Spirit bring them all to remembrance. Some of the memories may be painful. Let the pain out. Ask the Holy Spirit to help you to forgive and release them one by one. Then pray as follows:

*PRAYER*

*My Lord and my God, please forgive me for offending you by having held offence in my heart against ... (name of person who has offended you) By my will and from the depths of my heart, I release ... (name of person who has offended you) today from all blame. I cancel every debt I have held him/her accountable for. I ask you to forgive those who have sinned against me just as Jesus asked you to forgive those who had sinned against Him. Please bless ... (name of person who has offended you) and draw him/her into a closer relationship with you. In Jesus' precious name I pray. Amen!!*

There may be times after this when thoughts of the offence attempt to resurface. Cast them out from your mind by speaking God's word to it and declaring your decision to forgive, aloud. It is the devil trying to drag you back to an unforgiving attitude.

## b.    Discern Correctly

We must be able to discern things according to the will of God and not by our emotions or how we feel. We are all accountable to God, first; then to ourselves, relations, neighbours and the church community as a whole.

A Christian brother and a married sister who were in the same church fellowship were having an innocent chat after church and at the end they hugged and said good-bye to each other. There was a busybody standing a distance away who happened to notice it. She jumped to the wrong conclusion and with a lying, wagging tongue went about spreading false rumours that they were having an affair. This innocent sister was so miserable and hurt that she could not study for an impending exam. She sought counselling and prayers, but she still could not cope with the situation because it affected her relationship with her family. Eventually, she left her husband behind and travelled abroad for a while. On her return, she left the church.

This goes to show how an offence can have a spiritual and psychological effect on a person. She mistrusted churchgoers and could no longer go to church. Her fellowship and spiritual life were ruined. We may not have literally murdered or attacked anybody. However, we should remember that bearing false witness and wagging a lying tongue can offend and wreck somebody's life, and that is just as bad as committing murder.

### c.     Have a clear conscience

*Renew your mind to conform to the word of God.*
*Think right so that you are in a right relationship with God*
*Live right and be at peace with others.*

We are told in Isaiah 26:3 that we will have perfect peace when our minds are stayed on Him. Philippians 4:8, *"Finally, brethren, whatsoever things are true, whatsoever things are noble, whatsoever things are just, whatsoever things are pure, whatsoever things are lovely, whatsoever things are of good report: if there is any virtue and if there is anything praise-worthy, meditate on these things."*

You must be in control of your thoughts. Be prayerful and hold every negative thought captive in Christ's name, **(2 Corinthians 10:57)**.

**We have to pray for divine wisdom to handle challenges that occur in our lives in a godly way so that the end result is not counter-productive**.

A person who is in the wrong can be on the defensive. We live in an age of technology where information is disseminated within seconds and also mismanaged to destroy others. As Christians, we need to be sensitive in dealing with delicate issues by seeking God's guidance. It is not right to malign people, whether they offend us or not. Instead, we need to pray for them.

Chapter

# 3

# OFFENCE WILL DISTRACT YOU

God has a predetermined destiny for each of His children. So He sets us on the correct path towards the fulfilment of that destiny. Satan's desire is to move us away from that destiny; he is continuously warring with us to drag us off that path because he does not wish us to prosper and be filled with the joy that God has planned for us. He does not wish us to praise and glorify God for His goodness. If we fail in life, are miserable and constantly moan and curse God, Satan is happy. If God gives us a vision and we are able to follow His path to achieve it, we never cease to praise and worship Him. Since the devil knows this, his aim is to frustrate us so that we focus on the problems and not on worshipping God. This distracts our attention and shifts our focus from the main issues that we should be concentrating on.

Offences can distract you from pursuing the following:
  a.  Purpose, Goal or Course
  b.  God-given anointing and power
  c.  Relationship with God
  d.  Release into higher fulfilment

## a.     Distraction from Purpose, Goal or Cause

A person who holds an offence to heart is extremely dangerous. Apply divine wisdom in dealing with such people. When you are at variance with someone, your heart beats abnormally when you see that person. Deal with the offence in the right way and move on, even if it comes from your spouse or family member. Offence can undermine your authority, status, position, respect and can prevent you from reaching your destiny. That is why it is best to ignore the actions of people who offend you. If an offence is grave and affects you emotionally, you may react in a way that shifts your focus from your vision, totally. If you focus on the offence, your time and energy is virtually wasted on a totally useless purpose.

You limit your focus when you brood over an offence. You become selfish and self-centred. Fear takes over your life and you become suspicious. Walk away from offence even when it makes you feel defeated.  So what? Let people think what they like. If you give the devil attention, he will give you direction. Remember that the battle is the Lord's. The Bible says in Isaiah 59:19 that *"When the enemy comes in like a flood, The Spirit of the Lord will lift up a standard against him."* Let God fight your battles.

*"You have been raised to life with Christ, so set your hearts on the things that are in heaven, where Christ sits on his throne at the right-hand side of God. Keep your minds fixed on things there, not on things here on earth."*

Colossians 3:1-2.

Paul said in Galatians 2:20, "It is no longer I that live but Christ that lives in me." 'If any man is in Christ he is a new creation."

**(2 Corinthians 5:17).** Christ is in control of your life, do not allow offence to distract you, so you can achieve that goal or vision that is set before you.

Be like the songwriter who says:

*I'm pressing on the upward way*
*New heights I'm gaining every day*
*Still praying as I'm onward bound*
*Lord, plant my feet on higher ground.*

Chorus:
*Lord lift me up and let me stand*
*By faith on Heaven's stable land*
*A higher plain than I have found*
*Lord, plant my feet on higher ground.*

We need to sing:

*We've been made more than conquerors*
*Overcomers in this life*
*We've been made victorious*
*Through the blood of Jesus Christ.*

We need to be planted on higher ground spiritually so that we shall be able to ignore things that offend us. Let's examine how Christ dealt with offence: the Pharisees tried on several occasions to offend Jesus but whenever they tried, Jesus ignored it or rebuked them and foiled their plans. If Jesus had allowed offences to distract him, He would never have died on the cross to fulfil His destiny or goal to save mankind. When Peter tried to dissuade him from teaching about His death and burial, Jesus promptly rebuked him saying, "*Get behind Me Satan! You are an offence to me; for you are not mindful of the things of God, but the things of man.*" But only a few verses before that, He had said to Peter that he would be the rock on which He would build His church. (Mathew 16:18,23). I wonder how many people would turn up in church ever again if their pastor ever called them "Satan!"

The disciples asked for abundant grace to forgive those who offended them. You and I need the same measure of God's grace because it is certainly not easy to love our enemies. No human being is perfect. Everyone has flaws and that is what makes it difficult for us to forgive and love someone we know is plotting evil against us and wishes for our downfall. That is a real tough challenge, but we have to live by the commandment to love our enemies and pray for those who persecute us. The word of God admonishes us to "*Put off, concerning your former conduct, the old man which grows corrupt according to the deceitful lusts, and be renewed in the spirit of your mind* (Ephesians 4:22-23).

### b.    Distraction from God-given anointing and power.

Learn to overlook offences and do not allow them to consume you. We are all likely to offend each other, knowingly or unknowingly, at a point in time. Anyone who overlooks offences stands a better chance of being successful in life. You may have hurt more people than people have hurt you. You could even be offended by a sermon.  The way you walk may even offend someone, the way you dance to glorify God or your passionate utterances in response to a sermon in church could also offend someone who prefers a quieter form of devotion.  Take no offence when someone gets upset with your style of worship because it can easily distract you from receiving from God.

In the account in 2 Samuel 6:12-23, when the Ark of the Lord was on its way to Jerusalem, all the people of Israel danced and rejoiced at the sound of the horn. David danced before the Lord with all his might and was girded with a linen ephod. His wife Michal saw him leaping and dancing and was horrified at the way he danced, not caring that his clothes were falling off him. She took offence at that and she despised him in her heart. She thought it was dishonourable for a king to dance in that manner, even before God. David replied her, *"I will make myself yet more contemptible than this, and I will be abased in your eyes"* And Michal the daughter of Saul bore no child to the day of her death. The incident is an example of the critical and condemning attitude of a spouse. David did not allow expectations of how well a king should behave, to prevent him from dancing to worship and honour God. No wonder God blessed him so much.

### c.    Distraction from Relationship with God.

Samuel was the one who anointed Saul to be king of Israel. However, we read in 1 Samuel 16:1 that when God rejected Saul as king, Samuel mourned a great deal and was in danger of becoming distracted. Samuel had become so familiar with Saul that he could not accept that God had rejected him. He mourned until God himself asked him for how long he was going to grieve over Saul's rejection? When Samuel stopped and filled his horn with oil, he crowned a better and stronger king. Samuel overcame the pain and did not to allow his relationship with Saul to be a hindrance in his work for God.

Offence hinders the flow of the anointing. The anointing, the power and the breakthrough you want will not be released upon you until you have repented and your spirit is clear of offence. I cannot stress enough that as long as you remain upset, frustrated, bitter, disgusted etc. the Holy Spirit cannot accomplish His work in you. If you harbour grudges, the enemy will inhibit you. As we know, until Samuel stopped mourning over Saul, God did not give him any anointing greater than he had before he was assigned to anoint Saul.

Associate with those who have the right spirit. By this I mean people who do not harbour grudges. Find friends in objective and forward-looking people, who are constantly full of joy and encouragement. The man who has a contrary spirit will always seek harm or seek to destroy somebody deliberately.

**Friendships, relationships, acquaintances, anybody and anything must give way to your relationship with God.** Walk in the will of God. Follow God's direction, but stay away from anything that will drag you away from your God-given purpose. Be careful that nobody pulls you away from your destiny.

In **1 Samuel: 17: 26-29**, David could have vented his anger on his brother Eliab for his offensive behaviour towards him at the battlefield, but he did not allow himself to be distracted. Sometimes the wrong choice of words can be offensive. This can lead to an action which could undermine your credibility. Be careful of the answer you give when someone wants to deliberately offend you, because this could push you to react in a negative way and lead you to sin. In such situations, keep a handle on your emotions and sing songs like:

*Blessed be the name of the Lord*
*Blessed be the name of the Lord*
*Blessed be the name of the Lord most high*
*Blessed be the name of the Lord*
*Blessed be the name of the Lord*
*Blessed be the name of the Lord most high*

**Chorus:**
*The name of the Lord is a strong tower*
*The righteous run into it and they are safe*
*The name of the Lord is a strong tower*
*The righteous run into it and they are safe*

What people say about you does not matter; it is what God thinks of you that matters. People are subject to their own opinions and conclusions. What is God's opinion concerning you? Sometimes it takes someone to be offended with our mannerism just so that we may mature and receive our blessings from God. In everything and in all your ways, acknowledge the Lord and let your spirit be open to Him so that He can direct your path (Proverbs 3:6). If someone is jealous of you or offended at you or when the one bears you a grudge, you would be better off not wasting your time trying to change their perceptions, because you cannot and you might end up getting distracted from what God has in store for you.

Where there is nothing more you can humanly do to rectify a situation in which you have caused offence, after you have genuinely apologised, you need to keep away. Just leave it to the Holy Spirit to minister healing and peace to the offended person because at that stage whatever you say or do will not help, and you will only dig yourself in deeper. Sometimes, it is not that you have actually caused any offence, but people will be offended with you simply because God has elevated you above them.

### d.    Distraction From Release into Higher fulfilment

Jesus was hailed as The Messiah, King of Kings, Rabbi, Son of God, Teacher and Lion of Judah by strangers but, when He went back to His hometown, His own received Him not but they rather made reference to him as the carpenter's son (Matthew 13:53-58). *"And they were offended at him, But Jesus said unto them, 'A prophet is not without honour, except in his own country, and in his own house.'"*

Jesus Christ had performed miracles in other places and looked forward to coming home to introduce his folks to the glory of God. However, because of the wrong attitude of the people at home, they could not receive the glory.  Those who were around when Jesus was doing the miracles were only interested in His background, hence the reference, "Is not this the carpenter's son?" However, he never lost sight of His greater assignment and the glory that lay before Him.

Imagine what His mother Mary may have gone through when she was pregnant with Him, claiming that she had been impregnated by the Holy Spirit. Imagine the gasps, jokes, rumours, taunts and gossip that may have been directed at her. Mary had been a brave teenager who neither allowed any of the insinuations cast at her to detract her from her faith in God nor divert her attention from her destiny. Besides that, Jesus was now claiming to be the Son of God. He was not disturbed or distracted by the labels or His background just as His mother Mary had refused to be disturbed and distracted from the truth, because she knew she had a personal relationship with God. Instead she rather praised and thanked God.

Dear friend, gossip and insinuations mean nothing when you are focused on Jesus. Is your challenge your limited education? Or are you an unmarried mother? Do not let anybody distract you with an offensive word or deed. Sing to yourself songs that will remind you of God's power such as, "*All hail the power of Jesus' name*" and "*He's got the whole world in His hands.*"

Jesus offended quite a number of people not because of any 'abomination,' 'stolen something' etc, but because He had become a public figure and a prominent evangelist. Some were offended because God had lifted Jesus whom they had known from childhood above them. Instead of Jesus responding to their hostilities, He rather moved away and did not perform any miracles there. A person living in the flesh would have stayed there trying to prove himself to them. Jesus' example should teach us that this is the wrong approach. With time, the same people who are offended about your blessing will have no choice but to recognise and accept your greatness. Sometimes, there are people who will be with you or hang around you so long as you are 'ordinary' or a 'nobody' but as soon as you are successful and begin to prosper, they become jealous and despise you. Persevere and keep your focus on God. Every morning sing songs like this to yourself and stir up your spirit:

*I'm gonna stay right under the blood*
*I'm gonna stay right under the blood*
*I'm gonna stay right under the blood*

*Halleluyah, and the devil can do me no harm*
*No harm 6x*
*Halleluyah, and the devil can do me no harm*

Jesus was wounded but He knew what the purpose of God for His life was, so He was not distracted. He knew that *"weeping might endure for the night but joy comes in the morning."* He knew they despised and doubted Him. He was called a mad man, a demon and liar and other derogatory remarks were made about Him. Mark 3:21 says, when *"His own people heard about this, they went out to lay hold of Him, for they said, **He is out of his mind.**"*

His family and friends, brothers and sisters who were supposed to comfort Him said he was out of His mind. The scribes said he was possessed by Beelzebub and that by the prince of demons He cast out the demons. He was offended and bruised but that did not distract Him.

People may have doubted and despised you. Only you know how painful an experience it is. They have called you every name they can think of. Take no notice of them. Whatever God has said concerning you will surely come to pass. Like Jesus, do not allow anyone to reduce you to nothing. Do not be disheartened. All the people calling you those names are probably people whose names will not be heard of anymore as happened to Eliab. It is also said in Exodus 14:13-14, that, *"The Egyptians you see today, you will see them again no more. The Lord will fight for you, and you shall hold your peace."*

I Peter 4:12-15 states, *"My friends, do not be surprised at the painful things you are now suffering. These things are testing your faith. So do not think that something strange is happening to you. When people insult you because you follow Christ, then you are blessed. You are blessed because the glorious Spirit, the Spirit of God is with you."*

God called you, chose you and sanctified you for His own purpose. So if people do not understand you or your calling, just leave them to their own opinions and do not be offended. Do not live your life by people's opinions, and do not allow them to control you. You have the right to win the battle. You have the right to rise above situations because you are a child of God. You have the right to shake the dust off your feet. When you develop a Christ-like spirit, you will be able to stand against the wiles of the enemy that seek to distract you from the vision that God has given you.

Consider the story of Joseph and his brothers in the Bible. Watch out and stand against offence which is the bait of the devil. The enemy can use anybody to stir up discord which will cause you to lose your anointing. Pray and ask God to protect you and keep you from yielding to the temptation of retaliation.

**HOW TO AVOID DISTRACTION**

In the light of the various potential sources of distraction, the following measures are useful in counteracting them.

**i.    Do Not Lose Your Focus**

It is easy to lose sight of what God is preparing or using you for and be distracted by what you think others are not doing right. In Numbers 11:25-29, when Joshua saw two elders who had Moses' anointing prophesying in the tent, he took offence and went to Moses for permission to go and stop them from prophesying. Moses ignored it but rather said to Joshua that he wished God would give his Spirit to all his people and make them all prophesy. This is a clear manifestation of jealousy and it is purely a distraction.

In Mark 9:38-40, the disciples of Jesus were jealous and offended that somebody was casting out demons in His name and so they told him to stop because he did not belong to 'their group.' Jesus' response to their concern was, *"Do not forbid him, for no one who works a miracle in My name can soon afterward speak evil of me. For he who is not against us is on our side."*

Your gifting may be the subject of offence in someone's life and may be enough cause for them to place obstacles in your way or try to prevent you from using it. You do not need to pay attention to such things. Instead, you need to stay focused because it is the bait of the enemy. By yielding, you will get distracted and end up losing your anointing and fellowship. Do not be distracted by their negative reports or cynical remarks. Isaiah 53:1, says, *"Who has believed our report? And to whom is the arm of the Lord revealed?"*

Moses had sent out leaders to go and spy out the Promised Land. The story of Joshua and Caleb shows how the negative report by the majority is sometimes perceived as the truth. In Numbers 14:10, the people of Israel took offence at Caleb and Joshua and even tried to stone them for encouraging them to go ahead and possess the land. This was because Joshua and Caleb perceived the situation differently. They gave a positive interpretation to what they had observed and were not distracted from their vision of God's power. The others focused on the physical things they saw. As a result, God made sure that Caleb and Joshua were the only people from that generation who went into the Promised Land. All the rest died.

The majority view may not always be right. Remain obstinately in line with what you believe to be God's leading, especially if you are confident it is consistent with the word of God. If your efforts or views are not recognised, take no offence because your responsibility is to Christ who has called you and not to man. *"And whatsoever ye do, do it heartily, as to the Lord, and not unto men"* (Colossians 3:23). Pray about any hostilities and take no offence. Continue to do the work that God has given you to do and develop a passion for doing it. The words of this children's song come to mind:

*Dare to be a Daniel*
*Dare to stand alone*
*Dare to have a purpose firm*
*Dare to make it known*

**PRAY THE FOLLOWING PRAYER:**
*From today I refuse to be*
*Offended by the devourer;*
*Distracted by my enemies;*
*Destroyed by what I hear; or*
*Destroyed by my offenders;*
*In the name of Jesus. Amen*

## ii.    Keep your relationships in perspective

In Mark 3:31-35, Jesus refused to be distracted even by His own mother, brothers and sisters.  He had to neglect his own mother, brothers and sisters at that time by refusing to attend to them in order to do God's work.  Sometimes we have to disagree with those close to us in order to be able to move forward in the direction that God is leading us.

In the book of John 11, Jesus had a good relationship with Mary and Martha, but He did not allow his close relationship with the two sisters to distract him from His God-given mission. They expected Jesus to respond to their needs and anxieties and to be there for them all the time by virtue of their friendship.  They got offended when Jesus did not fulfil that trust.  When their brother was dying, they sent a message for Him to come. Jesus did not come on the first or second day. When He eventually showed up, they said to Him in their grief *"Our brother is now dead but if you had come earlier he would not have died."*

Jesus asked them to go and show him where Lazarus had been laid. Mary and Martha continued to moan about His delay in coming to them. However, He did not allow their concerns or complaints at that time to distract Him, even though they were obviously offended. Jesus had to disregard their emotions because He knew that it was impossible for them to reason as they were consumed with such grief and He understood their grief. No matter how intelligent you are, when you get offended and allow your emotions to get in the way, you temporarily lose your ability to reason soundly.

Jesus knew that Lazarus' illness and 'death' were for the purpose of glorifying God and so He did not allow the offence to sidetrack Him. The power of God raised Lazarus from death. God can resurrect our dead situations in the same way and bring back to life what is even decomposed. (NO MATTER THE INTENSITY OF THE ACCUSATION OR PERSECUTION RAISED AGAINST YOU WHEN THE POWER OF GOD SETS YOU FREE, YOU WILL BE TOTALLY FREE AND RESTORED AND YOUR ACCUSERS WILL SWALLOW THEIR WORDS AND BE FORCED TO CHANGE THEIR MINDS CONCERNING YOU). At that point, whether your accusers like it or not, they have to acknowledge God's great work in your life and glorify Him. As it is stated in Psalm 23, a table will be laid before you in the presence of your enemies and your cup will run over. They will have no choice but to admire God's hand in your life. We must always trust Him whatever the circumstances and be confident that:

*When we walk with the Lord*
*In the light of his word*
*What a glory he sheds on our way*
*While we do his good will*
*He abides with us still*
*And with all who will trust and obey*
*Trust and obey*
*For there's no other way*
*To be happy in Jesus*
*But to trust and obey*
**Also remembering that;**
*Everywhere he went*
*He was doing good*
*The mighty healer*
*He healed the lepers*

*When the crippled saw him, they started walking*
*Everywhere He went my Lord was doing good*

**Finally, we should not forget that:**
*He's got the whole world in his hands*
*He's got the whole world in his hands*
*He's got the whole world in his hands*
*He's got the whole world in his hands*

### iii. Look beyond the Horizon

Times and situations change: the environment changes and
society is dynamic. Nothing is static, so you must also change.
Do not allow offences of the past to continue to hold you in
bondage. You must be particularly sensitive to any change in
direction that is coming your way. Do not rely on your own
intellect. If you continue to brood over negative things of the past
that have caused you hurt and pain, anger or sorrow, you will
never become a better person. What was offensive to you in time
past may not necessarily offend you after a while.

> *In Luke 17:6, Jesus said, "If you have faith as a mustard seed*
> *you can say to this mulberry tree, be pulled up by the roots and*
> *be planted in the sea, and it would obey you".*

Your faith in God can help you stand firm against the trials of the
enemy and you will not be frustrated or take your frustration out
on others. Frustration is a killer disease and so is worry; so cast
them out from your life with all the trials and offences - past and
present - so that they do not interfere with your vision. God has

greater things for you in life. It does not matter what surrounds you. The Bible says that those who wait upon the Lord shall renew their strength and they shall mount high with wings like eagles (Isaiah 40:31).

Eagles and elephants are very powerful creatures. When they give birth their young ones are able to retain the scent of the environment in which they were born for several years. In that way, whenever they move away from their environs they are able to sense and smell their way back to the place of their birth.

Most of us go through pain because we go in the wrong direction. We do not exercise the gifts in us well enough to be able to discern and recognize the threats that certain situations pose. We are not sensitive enough to discern what the Holy Spirit is saying or the dangers in the logic, the rudiments and the philosophy of men. We do not understand the system of the world we live in. No matter what happens to you, do not be moved because the God you serve made provision for you before you were born. The most important thing is that there is something in you that needs to be developed. Do not dwell on offences, but move on with the times. The words of the following song would minister appropriately here:

*Be still and know that I am the Lord*
*Be still and know that I am the Lord*
*Be still and know that I am the Lord*

*You are the Lord that healeth me*
*You are the Lord that healeth me*
*You are the Lord that healeth me*

*I am the Lord that healeth thee*
*I am the Lord that healeth thee*
*I am the Lord that healeth thee*

All those negative things that have happened to you in the past or things happening to you now could easily offend and distract or ruin you. Say to yourself, "I am moving on." Change course if you want to receive that fresh anointing.   The enemy must not continue to keep you on the wrong path. If you allow people to manipulate and offend you, you will come to realise that you have been derailed from your course.

## iv.    Keep the Right Relationships

You must also be more discerning with whom you discuss God-given visions and plans. The wrong audience will not respond the way you expect if they do not understand you. In other words, do not lay your pearls before swine lest they trample over them and tear you in pieces (Matthew 7:6). Know when and how to open your mouth. Any offensive remarks from the wrong audience can make you angry and affect your relationship with God.

- Choose carefully those you call your friends. The Bible says a wise man chooses his friends (Proverbs 13:20).
- Choose those whose lives can change and motivate you.

Make sure you choose and walk with the kind of people who have the vision to encourage you on your journey of faith. Avoid those who will always offend you and lead you into sin or those who will become a hindrance. You need people who are optimistic, who can see the potentials ahead and are also prepared to move with the times. Proverbs 27: 17 tells us that, *"As iron sharpens iron, so a man sharpens the countenance of his friend."*

You have to have an assignment in life. Life without a vision or proper direction is fruitless. The devil seeks to destroy our vision and has many ways of destroying our faith to make us lose our focus. A distracted man cannot focus clearly. Never concentrate on your weakness, but on your strength. The power of God will give you the victory to overcome your weaknesses. Never waste your energy in trying to copy something someone else does better. Develop your own special and unique gift. To receive your miracle and promotion from God, you will need to drop any baggage that is dragging you backwards or down. However bad the experiences you have had, do not let them hold you back. Rather derive strength from them.

Love people and maintain a good attitude; but walk away from bad influences. Sometimes you need to make tough choices. Do not be tempted to take any course of action out of anger when you are offended as you are likely to make wrong choices and take bad decisions because your emotions are ruling you at that time. For example, violence breeds violence. God watches you to see how you respond to or handle offences. People can sometimes make things harder for you, if you do not handle matters well. The person that is dragging you down or distracting you may be your spouse, co-pastor, friend or somebody close to you. When love grows cold, one party can become vindictive and destroy the other. When you are a victim, do not allow the offence to poison you and make you negative. Do not focus on the pain and do not retaliate. Life is too short. Remember that you are a child of God and that He is looking after you.

Avoid ungodly counsel from unwise people who will fan the flames in a volatile situation and goad you on to actions that will cause you to disobey God. Prayer will help you to see people as they are, discern right from wrong and understand things from an enlightened angle.

Moses chose Joshua who proved to be the right person - one who was loyal, serviceable and honest. Joshua had a very good servant/master relationship with Moses. He knew all about the temperament of Moses, but he served him and remained loyal and obedient to him. God rewarded him and used Moses to impart his anointing upon Joshua. After Moses' death, Joshua became a notable leader who did many exploits (Deuteronomy 34:9). Pastors, associates pastors, assistant pastors and leaders should endeavour to work together in harmony and resolve issues among themselves amicably instead of fighting each other. Leaving one ministry to start another because you have been offended or because of failure to resolve issues, amounts to disobedience to God.

The world is made up of different kinds of people with various characters. Jesus' choice of disciples reflected this variety. Those He chose from different backgrounds worked together in unity to achieve the goal of ministering. They were able to do so with the help of the Holy Spirit which enabled them to put aside their differences and work for the common good. In doing this, aspects of their character changed, thus confirming the power of God to transform people. Peter had a problem with his 'mouth'. He often spoke without thinking first. Thomas was a skeptic, Matthew had been 'dodgy' in his financial dealings and James and John were over-ambitious and fanatical with fiery characters. But these men became united, acted with one accord, brought us the gospel and accomplished many miraculous feats. Their shortcomings may have been offensive but He was not distracted by them; instead He mentored them and always showed them love. Jesus has given us an example to follow.

God sometimes for His own purposes, brings people our way whom we do not like or get on well with. They may be irritating or a thorn in our flesh but, we should thank God because they usually turn out to be a blessing. God uses them to teach us certain lessons like patience and love, which we need to nurture as Christians, to fulfil our missions, to be able to handle certain situations and also to draw closer to Him.

For example, Judas had to be around Christ for a purpose and that was for Christ to fulfil His destiny. Pray for God to help you and give you the grace to be able to accommodate with love, those you do not like. The tares can grow with the wheat until the harvest (Matthew 13:25). The power of God transforms people. No man is perfect. Everybody has their weaknesses or shortcomings until God Himself begins to transform them into the vessel that He will use. Sometimes, the kind of people you want around you may not be God's choice for you. God looks into the hearts of men and women and sees more than we do. He sees the bigger picture that we do not see and we must have the faith to trust in Him.

## V. Be Confident and Contented

You must feel secure enough in your calling or in the plan and purpose of God for your life to be able to stand firm against distractions and attempts by others to hinder you. Adopt an attitude that asks itself, 'So what?' Human beings always find something to criticise. They will say you are too tall or too short, too fat or too slim, too miserable or too cheerful, too timid or overconfident, too quiet or too outspoken. You have to be something anyway. You cannot always win the praise of everyone so do not worry or take things to heart. Worrying will only raise your blood pressure and stress you out. It is wise however, to choose your associates carefully by asking God to intervene. It helps to choose people who are like-minded, people who think like you, believe in the same things, sharpen you up and believe in your cause. When they rebuke you, it is genuine and it is out of love. If you want to avoid being offended, get the right people as friends.

*What a fellowship*
*What a love divine*
*I'm leaning on the everlasting love*
*What a blessedness*
*What a peace is mine*
*I'm leaning on the everlasting love*

*Leaning, leaning, safe and secure from all alarm*
*Leaning, leaning, leaning on the everlasting love*

Offence is very distracting and can come from many sources. It is believed that the most common sources of offence in civil cases are those which are connected to family i.e. divorce. Broken homes are full of suspicion and betrayal. People from such homes reflect them in their outlook on life. They find it very difficult to trust anyone and are suspicious of everyone around them. Offences, when harboured, can distract us from our core purpose, our relationship with God and the things that can take us forward in life.

*PRAYER*
*If by any chance I am a victim of offence,*
*Lord sanctify me and restore my spirit,*
*So that I may remain on course to glorify Your name.*
*In Jesus name I pray. Amen.*

Chapter

# 4

# RENEW YOUR MIND AND OBEY GOD

Situations, events and the environment can influence our minds to react with emotions that can lead to offensive behaviour and attitudes. Our response to impulse and societal influences also plays a part in offensive behaviour. With offensive thoughts, we react to things and put up behaviours and attitudes that have damaging effects both on our lives and that of others around us; namely our relations, work colleagues, church members, neighbours, friends, acquaintances etc.

Spiritually, the human heart is corrupt as it harbours all sorts of negative traits. Trials in life will expose what is in your heart towards God or others. You either become bitter or grow stronger.

Jeremiah writes in Chapter 17:9, *"The heart is deceitful above all things, and desperately wicked; who can know it?"* Our minds are constantly under attack from the enemy. They are the battleground for the war between God and the devil. If the enemy can control our minds, then he wins the battle because that is where offensive thoughts (resulting in envy, bitterness, hatred and confusion) are generated. Once these thoughts begin, they start to affect your behaviour and attitudes. "*As he thinks in his heart, so is he*" (Proverbs 23:7). Once a man of God stated it like this: "*Your mentality determines your totality.*" Fortify the 'hedge' around your mind because Satan always seeks to make a hole in it. 1 Peter 5:8 tells us to "*be vigilant; because our adversary the devil walks about like a roaring lion, seeking whom he may devour.*"

Always take time to examine your thoughts, because your mind can be flooded with wrong thoughts that can serve as false witnesses and make you harbour hatred against people and prompt you to even go out to offend or attack them. Do your thoughts agree with the word? Psalm 119:105, advises us to let God's word be a lamp to our feet and a light to our path. Our belief systems, culture, society etc, shape and influence our thoughts as we grow up.

But when we become Christians, we are created anew in the Holy Spirit and must therefore begin the process of renewing our minds through reading and studying the word of God. Do you measure your thoughts against what is in the Bible or your own belief system? It is important to constantly renew our minds to conform to the word of God. As we do this, we mature and become more and more like the Father who adopted us and whose Spirit dwells in us. In the natural when we are born, we are like a blank canvass on which is then painted our character. We learn from our earthly parents and act and behave like them because they are our role models. Our personalities resemble theirs. In the same way, as we grow in the word and obey and apply it to our lives, Christ's character is reflected in us more and more.

In the next few chapters, I will be looking more at some of the practical issues and real dangers of offence in our daily lives and with reference to some prominent biblical characters.

We are all of different personalities and react to different things in different ways. Everyone gets angry. It is a normal human emotion, but as a child of God what counts is how well you are able to manage your anger when you are provoked. Different people resort to different measures to bring release to themselves in their anger. Some people will seek redress at all costs and take revenge, forgetting that they are supposed to be in Christ. Offence can lead you into litigation, using the Law courts to gain justice. People sometimes sue for libel or slander when they are wounded or their reputation is damaged.

Jesus understood and accepted offence as a reality of life. To His disciples, in Luke 17:1-5, He said, *"It is impossible that no offences should come, but woe to him through whom they do come! It would be better for him if a millstone were hung around his neck, and he were thrown into the sea, than that he should offend one of these little ones. Take heed to yourselves. If your brother sins against you, rebuke him and if he repents, forgive him. And if he sins against you seven times in a day, and seven times in a day returns to you saying I repent, you shall forgive him."*

And JESUS said "Forgive"

- o REMEMBER THAT, THAT WHICH WANTS TO PROMOTE YOU **WILL NOT OFFEND YOU**
- o ANYTHING THAT BRINGS YOU DOWN IS NOT FROM GOD
- o HOWEVER, ANYTHING THAT BRINGS YOU DOWN CAN BE USED TO PROMOTE YOU

**Avoid Hasty, Emotional Reactions**

When you are offended, it will make a big difference if you pause and reflect on the issue and God's grace for a few seconds before you react. Otherwise, you may become confrontational or display other kinds of behaviour which you will regret later on. Offence perpetrates violence and can also result in you losing your position, authority and dignity.

Miriam was Moses' big sister and a prophetess who led the women in praise and worship. In Numbers 12, she took offence because Moses married a Cushite woman (Ethiopian). Miriam and Aaron criticised Moses in anger. But God was angry with them, so He struck Miriam with leprosy for seven days. Moses prayed a simple prayer to God to heal her and she was restored.

Moses also behaved irrationally on certain occasions when he was offended. He sought revenge by murdering the Egyptian who killed one of his Hebrew people. As a result, he had to run away, and he became a fugitive in the land of Midian (Exodus 2:11-16). However, Moses came to repentance after the murder and God forgave him, hence his call and the prominent role he played as a leader of his people. In another instance, he became so deeply offended on God's behalf about the behaviour of his people on the desert that, in anger he smashed the tablet that had the Ten Commandments. The account in Exodus 32 records that the people had created an idol and were worshipping it in Moses' absence. He subsequently melted the golden calf the people had made, ground it into fine powder, mixed it with water and made them drink it as punishment.

Samson was an anointed man of God blessed from his birth, spirit-filled and a leader of his people. But he was "hot tempered" according to the Bible (Judges 14&15) and his anger, combined with his strength, was very intimidating. Samson took a Philistine woman as his wife against the advice of his parents. His father-in-law let him down later by giving his wife to his best man (a Philistine) in marriage. He took offence at that, and was furious and in his hot-temper went and took revenge on the Philistines by committing serious arson. He burned down their barns of corn and set fire to their orchards. He refused advice to "drink from his own cistern," took a prostitute and ended up breaking a whole city gate, to escape attack. As a result, Samson lost his anointing but, God being so kind, gave him another chance before he died. Samson was a great leader and a supernaturally gifted man of God, who failed to deal with his emotions and other weaknesses. His offensive behaviour turned violent and eventually brought ruin upon himself, his family and his own people.

Offence can make you act unintelligently and cause you to die a foolish death. God is a God of second chances who restores when you ask for His forgiveness and you in turn must forgive those who offend you. Do not allow your emotions to get the better of you. Make a real effort to deal with any uncontrollable temper. Ask the Holy Spirit for his help. Be angry but sin not the word says. Thank God there is hope in Him to set you free.

We read in Genesis 6, about how human wickedness angered God so much that He regretted creating man. The thoughts of man's heart was so evil continually that God decided to wipe man out by sending a flood to destroy the world, sparing only Noah and his family.

Noah was himself grievously offended when one of his three sons Ham, saw his nakedness in his drunken state. He was angry as he felt dishonoured by his son and so he cursed him (Genesis 9:18-28). It is believed, though controversially, that the black race descended from Ham and that the bitter words spoken over Ham by his father Noah have had a negative impact on the black race; hence the struggle and challenges black people face in life from generation to generation as compared to Caucasians.

A child of God should deal with offence in a godly way and not speak bitter words over people in anger, as we are all created in the image and likeness of the living God. Life and death are in the power of the tongue. We will all have to give account of ourselves to God one day for the curses we rain upon people who have offended us.

Bad behaviour is sometimes fueled by alcohol abuse which offends. It increases tension and friction in the home and can lead to destructive behaviour and cause damage to relationships. If you have a problem with alcohol, drugs or any other addiction, do not be in denial. Seek help so you do not damage your relationships through the resulting offensive behaviour.

**Manage Conflicts/Tension**

Paul and Barnabas were very close companions in the Acts of the Apostles. But they had their differences over John Mark. Barnabas wanted to take him along on the second missionary journey, but Paul disagreed because he was offended about Mark's behaviour and the fact that he had deserted them during the previous missionary journey. There was anger so Paul and Barnabas fell out with each other. Barnabas took Mark and Paul took Silas on their respective journeys. (Acts 15:36-40).

Barnabas was not heard of again. (He was known as the encourager who played a big role in the life of Paul after his conversion). The disagreement may have denied Barnabas the chance to be part of Paul's promotion and a position in his ministry. One can only speculate that God used Barnabas in a different way, but it would have been better if the disagreement had not happened in the first place, as it led to a broken relationship.

Paul was full of zeal and had no time for 'time wasters.' He encountered so many problems on his second missionary journey without Barnabas the encourager. They did not have such problems in the first missionary journey when Barnabas was with him. This confirms that teamwork is more fruitful than individual work. (One can cause a thousand to flee but two can send ten thousand to flight). However, Paul had a change of heart and there was reconciliation when he called for John Mark in his latter years of ministry (2 Timothy 4:11).

The situation where small misunderstandings lead to separations or desertions of pastors and leaders in a ministry is too common in our churches today. The hurt, sorrow and unforgiving attitudes generate bitterness that makes some of them lose their anointing and position. This has led to a huge number of churches springing up all over the place, borne out of conflict and with very small congregations. As a result of these conflicts and splits, many people even backslide and turn their backs on the church altogether. The enemy can also turn some who have remained into roots bearing poisonous and bitter fruit in the congregation. (Deuteronomy 29:18.) Reference can also be made to the bad behaviour of Diotrephes in 3 John; a leader who stopped people from coming to the church.

**Uncompromised Truth, an Offence?**

Jesus used very strong language in some instances to get his message across, which shocked and offended His disciples, followers, Pharisees and Scribes. He spoke about controversial subjects like breaking the laws of the Sabbath, the disciples not washing their hands, dining with sinners etc. (John 6:35-71). He spoke about being the bread of life, the manna that fell from heaven in the wilderness and also about the drinking of His blood. In verse 61, Jesus asked them, "Do you take offence at this?" We read in verse 66 that the disciples found His words too hard to swallow, for they did not understand Him and as a result deserted Him in droves. He turned round and asked the twelve remaining disciples, "Are you also going?" They turned to Him and asked him, "Where?"

The disciples had no problem in Jesus changing water to wine or even raising the dead, but when He challenged them with the truth they were offended. They murmured, disputed among themselves and then deserted Him.

Truth hurts and is not always pleasant to digest. People get offended when the truth is laid bare before them. It can bring hostility, desertion and retaliation in some form. Some people leave churches simply because the "unpopular truth" of the Gospel is preached. They prefer to go where the preaching is watered down or where the gospel is compromised.

Stephen was a man full of the Holy Spirit and of wisdom. He preached the Gospel in truth and performed signs and wonders. The men of the synagogue and other Jews took offence at him and Stephen was stoned to death. Saul before his conversion, was offended by the truth so he persecuted the church and consented to Stephen's death (Acts 6: 8-15, 7: 54-60). But what did Stephen do before he died? He asked Jesus' forgiveness for his killers. "Lord, lay not this sin to their charge." You and I should do the same to people who have offended and damaged us.

Paul was concerned about the Galatian church when he went back to visit because he noticed the church was living differently. Paul was offended that they were allowing preaching and doctrine other than what he proclaimed to be taught to them. He said to them, "Foolish Galatians, who has bewitched you?" In other words you started from the Spirit; you have seen the power of God; you have the anointing of the Holy Spirit; you have the flow of God; and yet still you allow evil communication to corrupt, pollute or spoil your previous good ways. Who has bewitched you? He knew they believed in God, they had the power of God and the Spirit of God in them but they were compromising the truth of the Gospel. (Galatians I: 6-10). This offended and angered Paul and hence his outburst over their ignorance.

When a wrong doctrine is promoted it can either set the body of Christ ablaze or paralyse them with fear and deny them the peace of God. One of the devil's strategies is to infiltrate the minds of preachers and introduce such false doctrines in order to deceive and draw Christians away from the truth. The doctrines he uses as bait sound so enticing, sensible, plausible and sweet that they are easily accepted as the truth. This is why we need the spirit of discernment. Ignorance can contaminate your faith and destroy your power and authority over the enemy and that was why Paul was offended with the Galatians.

Chapter
5

# A DESTINY KILLER

The book of Genesis (Chapters 37 to 50) narrates the compelling story of Joseph and the place of offence in the life of the man who rose from the pit and prison to greatness in Egypt. Joseph was the 11th son of his parents. He had a dream that he would become a very great man one day but, when he told his family about the dream they were offended. Joseph's dream sowed such seeds of discord, jealousy and hatred in his brothers that, they plotted to kill him. Joseph could also have contributed to the offence by being boastful in his attitude. He was only a teenager at the time, still immature in his behaviour but, he never lost sight of his dreams. In spite of all the hardship his brothers put him through and their evil acts towards him, Joseph had a free spirit and did not allow himself to be destroyed by bitterness. God used Joseph's experiences as a training platform for him.

The wealth of experience he gained in Potiphar's household (as a servant) enabled him to fulfil the destiny that God had for him. In retrospect, if his brothers had not sold him, he would not have had the training that eventually led to his being appointed prime minister. He would not also have gained the position that God had shown him in the dreams. It is important to have a broader perspective of the things God allows us to go through because He knows the bigger picture and we do not.

- The fact that people do not understand you does not mean God has not spoken or decreed that it shall be so.
- Not many people will share the vision that you have from God. His plan and purpose are for you and you alone. That is why He spoke to you and not to the doubters around you. He does not need their views or opinions on the issue to make the plan successful. He is the Author and Finisher of your faith and everything concerning you.

Whenever something comes your way to upset you, restrain yourself from reacting rashly and even if you are offended, do not allow yourself to sin. Don't be ignorant of Satan's devices (2 Corinthians 2:11). The devil baits and provokes you so much that you put away your self-control; you end up forgetting about your manners, your reputation and worst of all you put up unacceptable behaviours that have far-reaching consequences on your future or destiny. Constantly remind yourself that the Bible teaches us not to sin in our anger and not to let the sun go down on our anger or wrath so as not to give the devil an opportunity to destroy us (Ephesians 4:26).

You need to sow these **four basic things** into your spirit with the help of the Holy Spirit to enable you ignore offence and reach your destiny:
- Sow a thought and reap an act
- Sow an act and reap a habit

- Sow a habit and reap a character
- Sow a character and reap a destiny

If you put your trust and confidence in man instead of in Jesus, you will be disappointed and become a victim of offence all the time. The Bible says, "The arm of flesh will fail you," and "Greater love has no man... " Man can only do so much for you within the capabilities of his strength and power and beyond that you will be disappointed. The reason why some people get offended is that they rely so much on man. They look to men and put their trust in them forgetting that it is God who supplies all our needs.

Jeremiah writes in Chapter 17:5, "*Thus says the Lord, 'Cursed is the man who trusts in man and makes flesh his strength, whose heart turns away from the Lord. "* and Psalm 118:8 tells us that, "*It is better to trust in the Lord than to put confidence in man.*" You must guard against putting all your trust in a mortal man and placing him on a pedestal as though he is God. It is only then that you will save yourself from being disappointed and offended when he fails you. Ephesians 3:20 assures us that God is able to exceed our expectations when we recognise Him as the source of our provision. We will then be able to avoid some of the bad feelings and attitudes we display when we experience disappointments.

When Joseph was put into prison, he interpreted dreams for two prisoners who were connected to Pharaoh – the baker and the butler. Subsequently, Pharaoh executed the baker but, the butler was released from prison. Joseph relied on the butler and expected him to remember and give a recommendation for his release by Pharaoh. The butler however, forgot all about Joseph.

The Bible says that promotion does not come from man nor from the north, east, west or south (Psalm 75:6) but from God. There is nothing that we ourselves can do or arrange unless God himself approves it. The Bible says, until God gives, we labour in vain (Psalm 127:1).

I would not solely rely on man to recommend me. The man that you pour your heart out to and who recommends you from the flesh could be the same one who betrays you or stabs you in the back. But there may have been some people who have opened doors for you or directed you along a right path to achieving your goal, who themselves wondered why they did that. It is something that God himself had already ordained to happen, so when He instructs, there is nothing anyone can do to stop it. When he opens doors no man can shut them, or when he shuts them no man can open them (Revelations 3:7).

God loves us and in order for us to grow spiritually and know him even better, he sometimes allows persecution, frustration and challenges in our lives. These trials are painful and unpleasant as they offend, but they come into your life for you to realise that you have no strength or capability of your own. Then you turn to Him and He turns things around for His glory to be seen in you. Sometimes, we face trials and family and friends do not understand us just like Joseph, David and Daniel experienced. When you are falsely accused do you answer back or fight back in some way? If you are maliciously accused of stealing or doing something you have not done, what do you do? Joseph was falsely accused of rape and thrown into prison, a place of hardship and suffering. Joseph's experience in prison indicates that what God connected through you in pain will be a stepping-stone to the glory that is about to come. The pain or problem you experience is what God will use to open doors for you.

**Until you go through a test, you have no testimony.**

Naturally, Joseph must have been offended at the mistreatment from his brothers but, if he had sought revenge or harboured anger in his heart against them, his vision would never have been realised. Do you not think Joseph had every right to revenge against his brothers for selling him to strangers? He literally lost his identity as an Israelite or a child of Jacob. Genesis 41:45 records that his surname was changed to Zaphnath-paaneah when he naturalised, married an Egyptian woman and had two children by her.

**My prayer is that, no man should be able
to change your identity.**

When finally, God was about to work the miracle for Joseph, Pharaoh had a dream which all the magicians in the land attempted to interpret but failed. Then God acted by reminding the butler that Joseph (in prison) had a gift of interpreting dreams. So Joseph was called and he interpreted the dream. That is what brought him favour and immediate promotion from Pharaoh. This is an indication of how God allows breakthroughs to happen within His own timing and in accordance to His plan and purpose for our lives. And what could have been more telling than when Pharaoh himself recognized the excellent spirit in Joseph and said of Joseph to his servants, "*Can we find such a one as this is, a man in whom the Spirit of God is?*" Genesis 41:38. After that he made Joseph governor over all of Egypt as God had intended for him.

When Joseph's brothers eventually recognised who he was and remembered their hatred, mistreatment and betrayal of him, they were themselves afraid of his reaction. But Joseph reassured them with an amazing depth of maturity, saying, *"Fear not for I am in the place of God. As for you, you thought evil against me but God has turned it for my good"* **(Genesis 50:19&20)**. That was a perfect blueprint for handling a repentant offender. If Joseph had retaliated against his brothers, he would have lost out on God's reward and the privileges and blessings that came his way to benefit his brothers, father, their entire family and a whole generation.

When you respond sensibly with an assurance and confidence in Christ, regardless of the nature of the offence, then you are a winner. You become like a shiny star when you can ignore and overcome constant provocation, and conduct yourself with a Christ-like spirit, or when you act in humility. Philippians 2:14-15 reads, *"Do everything without complaining or arguing, so that you may become blameless and pure, children of God without fault in a crooked and depraved generation, in which you shine like stars in the universe."*

Everyone has been offended at one time or another and will continue to be, as long as we live on this earth. We must therefore be on our guard and take heed to stay humble so that we do not fall into sin when someone offends us. A man who is always offended and broken cannot see the glory of God or flow in the anointing. Men of God who continue to flow in the anointing are men who can move with the times and seasons, letting go of the past.

When the glory of God comes upon you, He uses the same old traits in you to speak forth His glory. God is no respecter of persons. If He wants to do something noteworthy or impressive, the Bible says He takes the foolish things of this world to confound the wise (1 Corinthians 1: 27-29). Quite often, we want God to do something and we want it within the time frame that we set but, God does things in His own time. You may not know how or when but, He will do it. Stop measuring God by time like the historians measure time. Judges 11 recounts the amazing story of Jephthah who teamed up with armed robbers after he was thrown out of the family home. In spite of his past, God made Jephthah the leader of the people of Israel where they victoriously fought their enemies.

*In His time, in His time*
*He makes all things beautiful in His time*
*Lord please show me everyday as you teach me your way*
*Just to do just what you say in your time*

You take offence because you do not know where God is taking you, i.e. His will for your life. What you see now is temporary; God is about to do something new and He is never too late. You may have been rejected and betrayed by men. People may have refused you certain things that might have helped you achieve a goal. That should not disappoint you or make you feel disheartened because your destiny is not in the hands of man. Remain steadfast and have a sense of willingness and a commitment to God like Joseph did, then He will use the dreams that He gave you in the first place to establish your destiny. You will then end up being a blessing to many, just like Joseph.

At the appointed time, God Himself will connect you to the right people for your vision to become a reality. Habakkuk 2:3 also says, *"For still the vision awaits its time; it hastens to the end it will not lie..."* When God has blessed you, no one can take the blessing away from you for the Bible says, *'They that know their God, they shall be strong and do exploits'*. All things work together for good to those who love God and are called according to His purpose (Romans 8:28). Anyone you know who does not celebrate your success is not with you but, that should not cause you to be offended or worried.

We read about the story of Balak and Balaam regarding the children of Israel in Numbers 23, 24&25. Balak, King of Moab, hired Balaam, the prophet of God, to come and curse the people that God had blessed because he hated them. Balak was jealous and felt threatened by the population growth of the people of Israel, and therefore took offence at them. As Balaam opened his mouth to curse them, blessings poured out of his mouth instead. Nobody can interfere with you as a child of God who has been blessed, because you have a covenant of victory with God.

**REMIND YOURSELF OF THESE:**
- **In your walk with Christ you need intercessors and not accusers**
- **Relationships are supposed to be based on respect and trust and not suspicion. Anyone who looks down on you is not on your side.**

God has given us grace which has nothing to do with who you are or where you come from; it is not dependent on intellectual ability, title, status or any other thing. It has to do with what God has purposed and it also helps us to live according to His will. **You can never receive grace if you do not recognise and accept it.** By the grace of God we are blessed and no one can curse us.

You are blessed beyond measure
You are blessed beyond imagination
You are blessed beyond the logic of men

**WHICH WAY?**
*Separation or Offence? (God's will or Satan's trap)?*

Sometimes God sets you apart for His own purpose. He may separate you from your own family and others to use you for a purpose which is ultimately a blessing to His children including your own people.

**Abraham was set apart by God** from his kindred and told to go to a land that God Himself would show him. He was also separated from Lot because of the quarrel between his men and Lot's but, this was according to the purpose and plan of God for him. He had to set apart Abraham for Himself in order that the glory of God would be seen in his life.

**Joseph** had to be set apart from his family and put through several painful experiences in order for his destiny to be fulfilled.

**Paul and Barnabas had to be set apart** from the other brethren, including prophets and teachers, by the Holy Spirit for God's use as missionaries (Acts 13).

**Esther was an orphan who was set apart** from her people in Judah and brought into exile by her cousin. God used her in exile to save the Jews from being exterminated. There are many lessons to be learnt in the Book of Esther.

Offence promotes disagreement between people, leads to hatred and can end in separation or the parting of company, as happened in the case of Paul and Barnabas over John Mark. If your friends or family reject and abandon you, it is naturally very hard to take, and the result can be devastating. You can become so offended that it can affect you emotionally, economically and spiritually, even to the extent of affecting your fellowship with God. A minor misunderstanding between you and your spouse or good friend can lead to a breakdown in the relationship, and it can escalate into something worse that will bring heartache and much pain into your life. Hatred, betrayal, suspicion, sadness and other negative emotions set in and anger, backbiting, malice, revenge etc. can result from it.

Make an effort to resolve disagreements and other issues amicably between you and your relations and friends to avoid long-term rifts. Relationships are valuable and are instituted by God; so avoid offence and pray for God to help you make changes that will enhance your relationships.

Bishop T D Jakes once said that, *"If you have been left behind, go your way and you will soon be the person leaving them behind."*

If you feel offended and wounded because you have been deserted, do not be discouraged or dispirited or lose hope, but hold on to Jesus because he offers reassurance, as you are precious to him. God is just separating you for a period. Elijah had done exploits for God by defeating the prophets of Baal but found himself alone in the wilderness, betrayed by his own people. He was offended and thought in his heart that God too had abandoned him. In that state of hurt and pain, he felt disillusioned, rejected and dispirited even as a prophet of God. If even Elijah could feel that way, how much more you and I? It is natural to sometimes have negative feelings. We should not let these overcome us. Elijah asked God to take away his life. **God came and assured him that he was not alone for He had seven thousand people alive in Israel who remained loyal to Him,** and so would support him **(I Kings 19:1-15).**

Paul was doing his missionary work but got offended and became abusive at the behaviour of his own people, the Jews, when he went to Corinth with the message. They opposed him and reviled him. He felt rejected and betrayed, so he shook off his garment over them in anger and chose the Gentiles thereafter. But God spoke to him in a vision to assure him that he was not alone, and that he should not be afraid but, rather he should speak and not be silent for, **"I am with you and no man shall attack you to harm you for I have many people in the city"** (Acts 18:11).

Perhaps you may be a pastor who is currently going through a very challenging situation in your church. The enemy may have instigated conflict, causing your members to leave you in droves. The ministry may be suffering as a result and you may be feeling badly upset. Do not take offence or be consumed with anger, worry or bitterness. Do not think badly of the people who have deserted you. They may have left because they do not form part of the next stage of the plan and purpose of God in your life. It could also be that God's assignment for them is finished.

In the ministry, you may have developed close friendship with certain people, invested so much in them and helped them in various ways, laid hands on them, prayed for their breakthrough but, they betrayed you and turned their backs on you. You had expected them to stand by you with prayers and to encourage you, but they have abandoned you instead. It is human to be offended when you look back but, ignore the hurt and do not be consumed with anger. Do not allow the bait of the devil to tempt you to revenge or to plunge you into depression over it and bring your spirit down. Do not sit in your corner and cry. Ask the Holy Spirit to help you overcome the negative feelings so that they do not wreck your fellowship with others and more especially, with God.

Naturally, not many people you started the journey of life with are able to come along with you till the end; some drop along the way. Not all the followers of Jesus followed him till the end; some deserted Him along the way. They all scattered in different directions when He was arrested including even the twelve disciples. Peter continued to follow Him but, at a distance while John remained with Him and followed Him right to the cross (John 19:25-26). Jesus felt the betrayal but, He continued to show love and forgiveness even till His death.

The journey of faith is not a competition. Nevertheless, it is like a marathon race where people need to use the spiritual muscles they built up as they run the race. Some people are left behind to build up muscles at their own pace. Paul said, "I have run the race...", so in the same vein, not all would come with you as you continue to journey along to where God is taking you next. God's will determines everything, and that includes those that will be of assistance to you on the journey for the fulfilment of your God-given vision or destiny.

David felt abandoned and betrayed when his confidant, Ahithophel, 'crossed carpet' to team up with his son Absalom, who had rebelled against him (2 Samuel 16&17). King David fell into such a state of melancholy, deeply offended and wounded, that he wrote in Psalm 55:13-14, "*But it was thou, a man mine equal, my guide, and mine acquaintance. We took sweet counsel together, and walked unto the house of God in company.*" David poured out curses because the man he trusted and considered as a bosom friend had deserted him.

You do not have to fall into the trap of the enemy and pronounce curses on those who have been disloyal to you or offended you. Be philosophical about it. It is part of life. Jesus set a good example, so I encourage you to follow it.

*My Prayer For You*
*May the Lord bless you*
*May the Lord heal your wounds*
*May the Lord lift you up*
*May every sickness bow in your life*
*We destroy every plan the devil has for you by fire.*

*May they disintegrate in the mighty name of Jesus.*
*May you not be a victim in any way*
*May the baits of principalities and powers loose their hold over your life.*
*May your spiritual eyes open*
*May your spiritual ears open*
*At the sound of your voice may principalities and powers have no choice but to bow.*
*May you see the land of the living and may you see the glory of the Lord*
*May that which God has purposed for you manifest in your life*
*In the name of Jesus*
*AMEN!*

Chapter
6

# OFFENCE – HAVE YOU PASSED THE TEST?

It is normal to expect a grave to be dug for our bodies to be buried in after we are dead. You thought you would be buried only when you died naturally but, people can dig your grave prematurely and bury you alive. This could be done by your pastors, church members, colleagues, family members, children, spouses, so-called friends and people you least expected. Gossip or evil reports, whether true or not, can affect a person's reputation in such a way that his career, ministry, social position, respect, business, marriage, relationships and whatever keeps them going could be destroyed. The person is brought low. This amounts to killing them whilst they are alive. It is even worse than physical death because the person has to continue to live with the situation and all the losses and humiliation attached to it.

*One day your faith will be tested.*
*One day your commitment will be tested.*
*One day your zeal will be tested.*
*One day the words you say will be tested.*
*They will all be tested*

We all experience offence one way or another but, do not be the one through whom others are offended. Jesus said in Luke 17:1, *"It is impossible that no offences should come but woe to him through whom they do come."* The Bible describes offence as sin. Offence is one of the things that the devil uses to steal God's glory from us. He always finds fertile grounds in the home, church, workplace, social environment, etc. to instigate offence:

- A husband rises up against his wife
- A wife rises up against her husband
- Children rebel against their parents
- Brothers revolt against their brothers
- Sisters revolt against their sisters
- Friends fight over shared benefits
- Church rises in opposition against their leaders
- Leaders revolt against the church's authority

**Despair and Disappointment**

John the Baptist played a crucial role in affirming the identity of Christ. In John 1:29-33, he heralded Christ's ministry and everything that Jesus was about to do. He pointed Him out to others. When it was time to baptise Jesus he said, "No, son of man, I am not worthy to baptise you," and Jesus said, "So the word of God should be fulfilled." When John baptised Jesus, the Heavens opened and God affirmed it by saying "This is my beloved son in whom I am well pleased." John was a witness to the light. His testimony was to glorify Jesus.

In spite of all these, when John found himself in prison he began to have doubts and lose hope and that was why he sent his disciples to go and ask Jesus whether He was the real one. His offence seemed to be at Jesus' apparent lack of concern for him. It will not always be as rosy as you think it should be.

Luke 7:17-23 records that John heard of the things Jesus was doing. John was languishing in prison and wrestling with his faith. He was probably confident that Jesus would support him, and expected him to just say 'the word' and he would be released, or use his power to bring fire upon those who had imprisoned him because He was the Messiah. John knew that Jesus had the power. Jesus did not act the way John expected. He had not even visited him in prison. This must have appeared to John as an act of abandonment, loneliness, neglect, despair and disloyalty. He began to reconcile the things that Jesus was doing (preaching, teaching and miracles) with what was happening to him.

What was worse, perhaps John heard that while he was condemned, oppressed and depressed in prison, Jesus was enjoying Himself. He was being told stories that were provoking, disappointing and misleading. The man he had spoken about seemed to be enjoying all the media attention. He was in the limelight and receiving rave reviews for his great miracles and messages. John and his followers had fasted because of Jesus, even though Jesus' followers did not really fast at the time. It seemed that whenever they heard of Jesus, he was always feasting. Even when there was no food, Jesus took a child's food and multiplied it to feed 5,000 men. You can imagine the anger in John's heart and his feeling of rejection and betrayal. John must have been offended because he was flesh and blood and was therefore demonstrating a natural human feeling.

Eventually, in his confused state of mind, he sent two of his followers from his prison cell to go and ask Jesus if He was the one who was to come or if they should look forward to another. Instead of looking towards God in the prison, John lost his peace and allowed the enemy to plant questions and doubts in his mind. Jesus did not take offence but said to them to go and tell John that the blind saw and the cripples walked. Take care that you do not kill tomorrow with the very thing you say today because of offence.

Doubts can lower your spirits, especially when after having done all you could as a Christian, including periods of fasting, nothing seems to work for you. It is even worse when it all seems to be going well for non-Christians and they seem to be enjoying themselves. You wonder if God is being unkind to you. You also wonder if He is 'sleeping' and whether He has even forgotten about you. This brings discontentment and discouragement. It is the trick of the devil, for he knows that when you begin to doubt, you cannot flow properly in the spirit.

Take courage and do not stumble, for God neither sleeps nor slumbers (Psalm 121:3). Unless you are careful, you could end up being offended with God Himself if you allow yourself to be absorbed into the whirlpool of logic. The man who does not believe in God appears to be enjoying himself and has a happy life but, you are still asking God questions and have no answers yet. What an irony!

You may be in a situation where nothing seems to be working in your favour. Your breakthrough might have delayed, with your personal circumstances seemingly deteriorating and your life taking a downturn. You may be irritated because other people are adding to your problems everyday. People may have laughed, judged you and called you names. You may even feel like going to ask them questions in order to explain yourself. It is not wise to do so, as they will not understand you but rather deepen your depression. God justifies and glorifies. Do not be offended. The adverse situation you are facing today is temporary. The devil's trick is to distract you from the beauty that will replace your ashes (Isaiah 61:3).

People who analyse you do not have the mind of God to know your future. Paul writes in 2 Corinthians 5:16, *"From now on therefore, we regard no one from a human point of view."* What God has in store for you, eyes have not seen, ears have not heard. It is best to talk less and listen more so you can hear what God is saying to you concerning your life and that is more important than trying to justify yourself before people, as that might be unwise and cause you more grief. Your faith is going through a test so take no offence: pass the test and receive God's abundance.

Beware of those people who offer you ungodly advice when you are offended, hurt and wounded. Many will come to gossip and massage your ego. Do not listen to them. They will keep you in bondage and prolong the offence and you will not be able to forgive and be reconciled to the offender. They will want to know if you are bothered with what that person has said or done to you. They will bring reports that will further inflame your wounds. Encourage yourself in the word. Do not wallow in a sea of negative feelings or hold a pity party. Some people will tell you, "If I were in your shoes I would do this or that." They are not in your shoes. Do not listen to the counsel of the 'Ahithophels' and people who act from their carnal minds. Psalm 1: 1-4, *"Happy are those who reject the advice of evil people, who do not follow the example of sinners or join those who have no use for God."*

The Birth of Isaac as narrated in Genesis 21, tells us very clearly that a little patience will bring you your miracle and breakthrough. Even though the suffering is long and there is a deep sense of despair, it is good to wait upon the Lord, for He will strengthen your heart and give you courage until His plan is accomplished.

**Wait on the LORD; be of good courage, and He shall strengthen your heart; wait, I say, on the LORD! (Psalm 27:14, NKJV).** For example, if you are trusting God for a husband and he has not yet appeared on the scene, wait patiently for the Bible says that even though the vision tarries wait, for it shall surely come to pass. Do not allow desperation, or frustration to drive you into a wrong relationship. Sometimes the delay is because God is preparing the man for you. God's time is the best; for in His own time, He makes all things beautiful.

In **Psalm 73,** Asaph the psalmist, was so offended with God that he became like Habakkuk (Habakkuk 1), complaining to God that He was silent and not listening to his desperate cries.

Anytime you get up in the morning, sing praises to the Lord. Wear the garment of praise. Asaph was the man who sang in the public place where David danced until his clothes fell off him. Some of Asaph's songs that David used implied that Asaph had witnessed and tested the power of God. However, when he had to wait, he became impatient.

If you are still waiting, then perhaps it is not yet the right time for you now. When the time is ripe, no agent, demon, principality, power, man, linguist, depth, things present nor things to come can stop it. When God's time comes, nothing can stop a thing from coming into being. Maybe God is preparing you for tomorrow and that is His way.

Habakkuk was serving God as a minor prophet. He complained when he had to wait. Stop complaining too! You already have a lot to be thankful for in life. Some people cannot walk, talk, have nowhere to live or food to eat. Habakkuk was complaining until God told him to shut up. This does not however mean that you 'shut up' due to ignorance of your rights and suffer in silence. Habakkuk's case was not one of ignorance. He knew the truth and acted otherwise.

A car knocked down a woman in 1989 in a country other than her own. Some men on the scene went to her aid. Her hips had dislocated. She declined any help and refused to visit the hospital. She claimed she was all right. It turned out that this was because she did not have a valid resident permit in the country. She was ignorant of the fact that she could still have had free emergency medical treatment. The enemy took advantage of her ignorance. The enemy always takes advantage of our ignorance.

Do not be like Asaph or Habakkuk. Do not allow a temporary setback to hinder your progress. Every negative thing you are going through today, definitely has an end. **Habakkuk 2:2** The Lord told Habakkuk to write down the vision He had revealed to him on a clay tablet, and that '*though it tarries, it will surely come to pass.*'

**Song**
*My faith has found a resting-place*
*Not in device or creed*
*I trust the ever-living one*
*His wounds for me shall plead*

*I need no other argument*
*I need no other plea*
*It is enough that Jesus died*
*And that He died for me*

Sometimes, it is easy to blame God or accuse Him of not answering your prayers when you have been waiting after much prayer. A little patience allows God's work, will and word to be achieved in your life. Know that God's ways are not our ways and neither are His thoughts our thoughts. John the Baptist was offended with Jesus, the Son of God and began to flag in his zeal so he could not spiritually link up with Jesus. He thought of how he had fasted and suffered and done all the forerunning for Jesus but, was left to his fate when he was imprisoned. This may seem a difficult advice to take but, learn not to be distracted by offences so you do not miss out on even your own inheritance.

John the Baptist forgot about his responsibility because of what he considered as an offence. His head (symbol of authority) was cut off and given to the stepdaughter of Herod. He died an unbefitting death. He should have been singing of Jesus, 'He is my everything.' Offence can make you lose your level of authority, calling, status or position. Your position will be given to someone else who may use this authority (that would have been otherwise yours), against you. You may not fully appreciate what you have today but, bear in mind that someone else desires it.

The story is told of a man who planned to hang himself because of poverty. He therefore took off his clothes and put them in a pile under a tree and prepared a noose that he was going to use to hang himself. Just as he was about to hang himself, he noticed a tramp collecting his clothing. He quickly abandoned the noose, chased the tramp and retrieved his clothes. This made him instantly aware that someone was worse off than he was. The incident made him change his mind and so he preserved his life.

Pray that anything that will make you loose your glory should pass you by. Your glory is too important to be sacrificed for just anything. Your glory is that unique thing that sets you apart from others and it is what makes you who you are. Your glory makes you that special person who cannot be compared with any other. Constantly ask God to help you not to be so offended that you lose your glory. You should also stay away from an offended man or woman because they can also cause you to lose it all. Refuse anything that has become an obstacle in your life. Tell the devil that you will not lose your guard anymore.

**Song**
*For I've been to many places*
*And I've seen so many faces*
*But there are times I feel all out there alone*
*But in my lonely hours*
*In those precious lonely hours*
*Master Jesus He makes me feel I am his own*
*I thank him for the mountains*

*I thank him for the valleys*
*I thank him for the storms he brought me through*
*But if I didn't have a problem*
*I wouldn't know that God could love me*
*And I wouldn't know what my faith in God can do*

**Chorus**
*Through it all*
*Through it all*
*I've learnt to trust in Jesus*
*I've learnt to trust in God*
*Through it all*
*Through it all*
*I've learnt to depend upon his word*

**Song**
*Captain of Israel's host and guide*
*Of all who seek the land above*
*Beneath thy shadow we abide*
*The cloud of thy protecting love*

*Our strength, thy grace*
*Our rule, thy word*
*Our end, thy glory of the Lord*

**Song**
*Some folks may ask me*
*Some folks may say*
*Who is this Jesus, you talk about everyday*
*He is my Saviour; He sets me free*
*He is my everything; Now what about you*

There are two things to consider:

- o Offences are supposed to make you vigilant and not to destroy you; so rather than dwell on them, concentrate on Christ's omnipotence, grace and goodness.
- o Offences are not supposed to direct your path. It is the Holy Spirit and the word that should guide you (Psalm 119:105. Psalm 19: 7-11). Learn to laugh at the devil. Sing hymns and songs of praise when you wake up in the morning,.

**You Have Authority. You are Above the Offence**

Deliberate and meditate on the following:
- o **There is a unique calling upon your life.** It has to do with your God-given personality and nobody can replicate it. The person distracting you from your goal cannot go where you are going.
- o **Your calling attracts Satan's attacks.** If you never face attack, then you are doing something wrong. The Bible says, *"Woe unto you when all men speak well of you"* (Luke 6:26).
- o **God requires you to be on your guard.** Sometimes you may find yourself in a situation where a storm seems to be rising against you. You sense that someone is intentionally provoking you. Put on the full armour of God so that when the day of evil comes, you may be able to stand your ground. Anything or anyone that will come to offend you is instigated by the devil. I want you to come to a place and a point where, if the enemy comes to your doorstep, you can confront him yourself with the sword of the Spirit - the word of God. You have power and authority over him.
- o **The devil does not work in a vacuum.** Your son, brother,

friend, husband, wife or pastor can provoke you to anger. The anger will be an open door through which the devil can attack you. Watch your words carefully when you are provoked, for words are spirit. Do not give way to the devil. *"The power of life and death is in the tongue."* If an outsider provokes you, it is not as painful as when someone closer does.

o **Whatever your gift is and however small you consider it to be, use it wisely.** Bear in mind that it is what you are holding already that God uses to bless you. This has nothing to do with education. Knowledge is acquired but, God gives wisdom. Some people have never had a mind of their own. They just follow the crowd and wherever the crowd leads them. They follow the broad road that leads to destruction, thus bypassing the narrow way that leads to their own fulfilment and glory (Matthew 7: 13).

**Song**
*I'm only human*
*I'm just a woman*
*Lord give me the strength to do everyday what I have to do*
*Yesterday is gone sweet Jesus*
*And tomorrow may never be mine*
*So help today*
*Show me the way*
*One day at a time*

You do not have to remain where you are today forever. You must progress in life and bear fruit. You are above offence but do not know it. You are like a person who has been left an inheritance but does not know it. You should be generating thoughts and ideas. Create a journal and write down your dreams and visions. See if they are in line with the word of God. Pray about them and ask God to direct you. Find Bible quotations that will encourage you. Follow your dream and back it up with much prayer. This will help you know your purpose in life. Do not let anybody divert your attention from your calling, beauty, glory, ability, gifting and strength because of offence. There is a special glory on you that is yours alone and cannot be acquired with money.

The reason why your miracle has not yet happened is that you are overly concerned with the trials and challenges you are facing, and blaming God. You are asking him, why me? Instead, try and:

o Focus on your strengths. Just be like the eagle.
o Do not compare yourself to anybody

**Song**
*I need no other argument*
*I need no other plea*
*It is enough that Jesus died*
*And that He died for me.*

We need to remember that arguments can arouse emotions. Anger can set in and you can lose your cool, throw your manners overboard and give the devil an opportunity to enter your life. Proverbs 14:17 reminds us that, *"A quick tempered man acts foolishly."* Offence can make you lose or lower your position or authority in the home, workplace or church. There is nothing you are doing right now that someone else cannot do better. This is because your success is by the grace of God and not by your own strength; you must never think that you are irreplaceable. Someone can take your position in the workplace and use it to your disadvantage.

One day a father was away on a business trip, and while his wife was chatting with their son the boy mentioned that a family friend, Aunty Sheila, had been visiting Dad when Mum was away. Mum questioned him further and he told her that they were usually in the bedroom talking and doing things. The boy's mother asked him to repeat the story at the dinner table that evening when his father was at home.

During dinner, the mother introduced a piece of conversation which led to that subject she had earlier discussed with her son. The son then narrated what he had already told his mother, about the visits of Aunty Sheila. Mother then asked him what they usually did. The boy answered innocently, "The same thing you and Uncle Sam do when Dad is not in." Imagine the mutual embarrassment of both husband and wife.

The result was a destruction of trust and the deterioration of the relationship. Neither was right but without the forced disclosures from the son they might have remained a happy family.

**Divorce over a game**

Another situation that resulted in divorce was one where a diplomat and his wife were playing the indoor board game called Ludo. The wife found herself losing every game. She began to observe her husband carefully and detected that he was cheating in the way he threw the dice. As a result, the numbers he needed for his moves were the ones that always came up when he threw the dice.

She was so furious that she lashed out at him verbally, calling him all sorts of unprintable names. He also retaliated and it became a very big quarrel with unrelated issues being brought in. They were both arrogant and neither could bring themselves to apologise to the other and come to a position of reconciliation. The result of this confrontation was a divorce. The enemy used what started as a game, a recreational activity, to destroy a marriage and whatever plans God had for the couple.

We must constantly be on our guard so that little or irrelevant things do not become the instruments that the devil uses to destroy us. The door that the devil used in this case was the dishonesty of the man. Although he used it only in a game, it was still deceit and had he resisted the temptation to cheat to win when the enemy put the thought in his mind, the whole incident would not have occurred. If the wife had also responded wisely to the husband's cheating, she would have avoided the trap of Satan to destroy their marriage.

### Song
*I have decided to follow Jesus.3x*
*No turning back. No turning back.*
*Take the whole world and give me Jesus.3x*
*No turning back. No turning back.*
*Though none goes with me, I still will follow. 3x*
*No turning back. No turning back.*

## Song

*There is a redeemer*
*Jesus God's own son*
*Precious Lamb of God Messiah*
*Holy One*

*Thank you oh my Father*
*For giving us your Son*
*And even your Spirit till*
*The work on earth is done*

## My Prayer for you

*May the Lord bless you*
*May the Lord keep you*
*May the Lord promote you*
*May your expectation not be cut short*
*May the Lord lift you up like the cedar of Lebanon*
*May you be planted by the river*
*May you flourish in everything you do*
*May you be blessed.*
*May nobody who is offended distract you.*
*In Jesus' name. Amen.*

Chapter

# 7

# SPARE YOUR ENERGY

- o What is it that has offended you to such an extent that you cannot let go?
- o Have you ever met a person who has never been offended?
- o Do you worry yourself about things that do not matter?
- o Do you unnecessarily stress your heart and cause it to beat abnormally?
- o Have you been striving to prove a point when you do not have to?
- o Are you over-concerned about what that brother or sister said?

There are many incidents that vex us and make us angry. We insist on the offender making it up to us in one way or another instead of leaving those matters to God. There is the case of a certain African clerk who beat up his wife because she found out that he had been having affairs and buying beautiful clothes for his girlfriends whilst neglecting her needs. She demanded that her husband buy her 25 traditional African cloths to pacify her for his philandering. This type of pacification was traditional in their culture. The husband refused and they argued and fought to the extent that their parents had to intervene in the matter.

If we understand like Jesus did that, offence, tribulation, attacks, frustration and peril will come our way, we can then determine in advance that when they come, we will ignore them and not allow them to affect us to any degree whatsoever.

Jesus speaking figuratively in Matthew 5:27-36 said among other things that, *"If your eye causes you to sin pluck it out, and if your hand causes you to sin cut it off."* In other words, ruthlessly remove from your life anything that leads you to sin. Do not compromise with it otherwise it will bring ruin to you and infect those around you.

Jesus warned his disciples about offences in Luke 17 1-5:
*"Then He said to the disciples, "It is impossible that no offences should come but, woe to him, through whom they come! It would be better for him if a millstone were hung around his neck, and he were thrown into the sea, than that he should offend one of these little ones. Take heed to yourselves: If your brother sins against you, rebuke him; and if he repents, forgive him. And if he trespasses against thee seven times in a day, and seven times in a day returns to you, saying, I repent; you shall forgive him."*
*And the apostles said to the Lord, "Increase our faith."*

Forgiveness is a very difficult thing to do in the natural. It is a painful, difficult, long and costly exercise. You may have to lose face when you seek to make peace, even though you may be in the right. The apostles walked and talked with Jesus and had no problem with Jesus cleansing the lepers, calming storms, performing miracles, raising the dead etc. The one thing they did have real problems with was forgiveness and that is why they asked for more faith to be able to deal with it.

Forgiveness is one thing that we all need to exercise. We therefore need to ask the Holy Spirit to give us faith to be able to do this, as Christ commands us to do. Everyone has been offended before and everyone has offended others at one time or another. I am sure that there is someone somewhere you wished you had never met; a person whom you once considered your best friend but has now turned out to be anything but a friend.

Psalm 55:12-14 points out:
*"For it was not an enemy that reproached me; then I could have borne it: neither was it he that hated me that did exalt himself against me; then I would have hidden myself from him: But it was you, a man my equal, My companion and my acquaintance, We took sweet counsel together, And walked to the house of God in the throng."*

David continues in verse 21 that:
*"The words of his mouth were smoother than butter, But war was in his heart; His words were softer than oil, Yet they were drawn swords."* He then advises that you *"cast your burden on the Lord, And He shall sustain you."* Quite often, it is only after man has failed us that we turn to God. We would avoid a lot of heartache if we did it the other way round.

Remember Jesus commands us to bless and not curse. May the Lord increase your faith. Remember also that none of the trials or difficulties you are going through now is permanent.

## Offence and Sickness

Offence affects your spirit, soul and body. It opens you up to heart problems, pain, depression etc. Because you live with and relive the offence, pain and hurt, your heart begins to pound whenever you see the person who hurt you. You look away, pretend to be occupied with something else or even jump onto the wrong bus or train just to avoid them.

The root of so many diseases is emotional hurt and failure to forgive. A great percentage of our ailments have their roots in offence. Offence can make you suffer from a stress-related illness. Your immune system easily gets affected. You can even suffer hypertension, or any such serious disease that can eventually kill you.

The Bible says that you need to remember that your body is the temple of God, so it is precious. The pain, embarrassment and bitterness that have taken root in you can kill you. I bind every sickness that is associated with offence! I pray that no sickness due to offence will remain in your body.

You have to cleanse yourself of all defilement of spirit and body for the blessings of God to flow into your life (2 Corinthians 7:1). This includes wrong and sinful attitudes, resentment, bitterness, malice, an unforgiving spirit etc. Jesus taught that it is not that which goes in but that which comes out of us that defiles us (Matthew 15:11). There is no point in forgiving the person who offends you when you still keep a diary or record of the offence. 1 Corinthians 13:8 stresses that *"...Love keeps no account of wrong doing..."* If Jesus loves me and keeps no record, then I must also love others.

Be of good cheer and do not allow anything to affect your countenance. Scientists say it takes more nerves and muscles to frown than to smile. Smiling itself is therapeutic. Frowning is disease (**dis** and **ease;** that is the lack or absence of ease within us) and sickness. The following prescription will help keep offence at bay:

- o Avoid anything that will bring offence to you.
- o Avoid anyone who will bring offence to you.
- o Never stay around anyone who you know wants to offend you.
- o Bear in mind that anything that brings offence to you can bring sickness to you.

You cannot expect God to hear your prayers when you are rooted in offence or when you are storing up anger and other negative emotions in your heart. David often exhibited the failings of human nature when he prayed prayers of revenge, fire and brimstone over his enemies. At times he cursed them, while he threatened others like Nabal. He acted out his human nature many times and sometimes behaved like a wimp, immersing himself in pity parties; even though he was a man after God's own heart.

Jesus was able to save mankind because he was sinless. He prayed on the cross for those who crucified him, saying *"Father forgive them for they do not know what they are doing."* Because we live under the dispensation of grace, we are called upon to forgive our enemies.

"You are a disciple of Jesus and He has, through His spirit, given you power and authority. Any bitter or negative words or curses you speak over anybody including your spouse and children will have a negative effect. The result of such words though spoken in haste and anger and probably, without malice are manifested in the spirit and could be fulfilled in the person's life. This is because you have opened the door to Satan to bring that which you have spoken to pass. All he needs to do is watch and wait for the right opportunity. When those words take effect in your loved one's life and they are suffering, your words will haunt you for the rest of your life. You will know that your pronouncements are responsible. Are you prepared to bear that? If not, curb your tongue and think before you open your mouth and utter any words, for you will give account to God one day.

Spend time to meditate daily on the scripture below and memorize it if you can:-

**Psalm 19:14,**
*"Let the words of my mouth and the meditation of my heart*
*Be acceptable in your sight, O Lord my strength and my Redeemer."*

If you want to move on fruitfully in life, spend more time on your knees. You may look stupid to some people or foolish at that moment but, do not let these bother you. Lift your eyes up to the hills. Your confidence is in Him. Do not take offence because of the situation you find yourself in. Since the challenges and storms of life are all temporary circumstances, avoid arguments with people. Leave them to their opinions. You cannot justify yourself to anyone until God himself justifies you. What God says about you is final and that is why you do not have to argue things out. Kill your inner pride that causes you to want to justify yourself.

*Moreover whom he did predestine, these He also called, whom he called, these he also justified, and whom He justified, these He also glorified. What then shall we say to these things? If God is for us, who can be against us?*
*He who did not spare His own Son, but delivered Him up for us all, how shall He not with Him also freely give us all things?* **Who shall bring a charge against God's elect? It is God who justifies.** *Who is he who condemns? It is Christ who died, and furthermore, is also risen, who is even at the right hand of God, who also makes intercession for us.*

Romans 8:30-34

There is the word posterity which means 'time will tell.' Stay focused, refuse to walk in offence and one day, those who were against you will:

- Swallow their words
- change their minds, and
- themselves confess what they thought of you some time ago

Then you will Sing:-

*Great is Thy faithfulness*
*O God my father;*
*There is no shadow of turning with thee*
*Thou changest not,*
*Thy compassions they fail not,*
*As thou hast been*
*Thou forever wilt be.*

*Great is thy faithfulness*
*Great is thy faithfulness*

*Morning by morning new mercies I see*
*All I have needed, thy hand hath provided,*
*Great is thy faithfulness*
*Lord unto me.*

Because you want to move on in life, leave the justification to God. Sometimes the hurt or offence is so deep that we wrongly take revenge even though vengeance is the Lord's according to the Word. There are battles we fight today that are not necessary. If you begin to fight a brother, you use your carnal human mind and worldly or political tactics. These will not succeed in winning that fight because you are using carnal weapons against a spiritual enemy. You should be using spiritual ones. Release yourself and invite God's spirit and when that is present, every knee shall bow and every tongue shall confess that HE is LORD. Just ensure that you continue to be in fellowship, showing love and compassion.

### PRAY THIS PRAYER:
*God help me not to take offence*
*God help me walk away from offence*
*God build a hedge of glory around my life*
*God help me to build a strong anchor in you*
*God help me in every way that I am weak.*
*In Jesus' name. Amen*

### Sing this song to acknowledge God's Mercies:
*Mercy rewrote my life*
*Mercy rewrote my life*
*I could have fallen,*
*my soul cast down*
*Mercy rewrote my life*

Avoid people who encourage you to overstep boundaries. Some people come to visit and fuel your anger concerning your brother. Avoid anyone and anything that may perpetuate the offence; for:

- It destroys faith,
- It worries you, and
- It destroys your confidence.

Preachers, you can never flow when you are offended. Nothing is more difficult than when, during your preaching, someone who is shouting "hallelujah" has said offensive things about you. You wonder whether they are being genuine or sarcastic. Do not allow people's attitude and criticism to offend you and cause you to change your testimony or ministry as long as you are doing things according to the will of God. Do not change your style to suit anybody; maintain the way you have been called to minister.

**Obedience**

In Genesis 26, Isaac wanted to go back to Egypt because there was famine but, God told him to stay in the land of the Philistines Gerar, where he would bless him greatly. That land was a place of constant opposition, enmity, quarrelling, etc. instigated by the Philistines but, God had promised to be with him. Isaac therefore obeyed God and stayed despite all opposition. God rewarded him by prospering him in that land, keeping the covenant He made with Abraham. Later on when Abimelech the king and the Philistines realised that God's hand was on him wherever he went and in whatever he did, he went and made peace with Isaac and they became friends. The obedience of Isaac resulted in the manifestation of his blessing. We should also learn to be obedient to God rather than deciding to do what makes sense to our carnal minds.

**Disobedience offends God**

*Samuel and the Rejection of Saul*
In 1 Sam 16:1, the Lord said unto Samuel, "**how long will you mourn for Saul, seeing I have rejected him from reigning over Israel?** Fill your horn with oil and go, I am sending you to Jesse the Bethlehemite. For I have provided myself a king among his sons."

Our disobedience to God offends him too but, he has his own way of dealing with it. Saul was an impressive king who towered in height over all his people, a man appointed by God himself. Everyone looked up to him as a leader. He performed his kingly duties well. He however failed to fully obey God's command and so he was rejected by God. In his own words, he made the mistake of fearing the people and obeyed their voice instead of obeying God. As a leader, he chose to bow to the pressures of the people and lost his crown as a result.

In 1 Samuel 9 & 10 apart from being Saul's mentor, Samuel had a good personal relationship with him. Saul was the first king of the people of Israel. Saul and Samuel related well together as a team. When God rejected Saul, Samuel had to make a very important decision concerning his walk with God and with Saul. We all have to make such decisions at certain times in our lives. Samuel was reluctant to make a choice. God had to remind him to act wisely. When forced to make the choice, his allegiance naturally was with God.

Samuel realised that if he continued to maintain that close relationship with the rejected King Saul at the expense of his responsibility to God, he might lose his position to somebody else (just like Saul had lost his to David). Remember that your friend should not be more important to you than God. "A live dog is better than a dead lion."

Be careful not to take the anointing of God for granted. Familiarity can quench the flow of God's anointing in your life. For example, if you are in a leadership role, as people are looking up to you, you have to look up to God. Bear in mind that God can humble you and exalt someone else into your position if you yield to pride. He chooses to do what He wants and shares His glory with no one. When God instructed Samuel to go and anoint David, he had to obey that. Note that if God gives you instructions to carry out and you fail to carry them out, it is an act of disobedience.

### Jonah's Diversion

Jonah was a prophet of God who decided to follow an agenda different from that which God had asked him to. He was refusing to go to Nineveh, choosing to go to Tarshish instead. Jonah was angry and was convinced that God would not carry out his threat against Nineveh. God was displeased with Jonah's disobedience and so he decided to punish him. God created circumstances which got him thrown out of the boat and arranged for a whale to swallow him. Amazingly, he did not die but that experience gave him time to reflect without distraction. He realised that he could not run away from God, so he repented. Once he repented, the whale vomited him out.

From this we should learn that:

- o When we disobey and try to take our own path to a destination different from God's, we struggle and the way is fraught with obstacles and difficulties. (It is as though God is laughing at us for trying to run away from Him). He lets us carry on for a while and then reminds us that He is still in control.

- o Jonah's story also illustrates God's great love by His willingness to forgive us when we repent.

## *Moses and the Rock*

In Numbers 20:7-12 Moses was instructed by God to take a stick and speak to the rock so that water would flow out of it for the people of Israel. Moses bowed to the pressures of the people whom he described as 'rebels' and instead of speaking to the rock he struck it. Although the miracle still took place and water came out, God was offended by the disobedience and vowed to Moses that he would never enter the Promised Land. Moses remained leader but he lost his promotion or blessings that would usher him into the next stage of their journey. This was in spite of all the exploits that God had used him to perform right from the time they left Egypt. Moses allowed the pressures of the rebels to get to him. After all his effort, he lost his ultimate reward of entering into and resting in the Promised Land.

If you are a pastor, leader or minister, do not allow yourself to be pressurised by the people. You cannot please everybody. You can become offended and lose your focus and the real threat here is that it can distract you from the work of God, affect your health and your general well-being. Many have given up their ministries altogether because they could not cope with the challenges. Just look to God for strength and direction as Moses did.

### Beware of Nahash the Ammonite

After Saul's anointing as king, something interesting happened in 1 Sam 10:27. The children of Belial refused to pay homage and asked, *'how shall this man save us?'* And so they despised him, and **brought him no presents**. But he held his peace. The rebels around Saul's leadership were unhappy at the choice of Saul as king because they had doubts about his military leadership. They were so offended they behaved contrary to the custom and gave him no presents on his coronation. Some people communicate their offence by withholding their offerings. They think that by giving offering they are doing the pastor a favour. However, a pastor who stands for integrity is a good steward of the money that he receives.

As a result of the refusal by some to acknowledge Saul's leadership, the front of the people was divided and full of offence. In 1 Samuel 11, the people of Jabesh Gilead were besieged by Nahash the Ammonite. Unable to defend themselves, they ceded their lives over to the devil by offering to sign a pact with the Ammonite king to become his subjects. God will still do for you that which He has promised. Don't give up on Him and sign an agreement with the devil instead. Today certain people are laughing at you but God is about to do mighty things in your life. Those people do not have the eyes to see or ears to hear what God has told you. They think they know your future. They think you are in a hopeless situation. God is going to make a way for you where there seems to be no way.

Beware of whom you submit to. The name 'Nahash' means a snake or serpent. Some people have some Nahashes lurking in their lives. Significantly, Nahash had realised that there was a seed of offence among the people and that they had become vulnerable so he was able to easily make them break their promise to God and their king. Nahash offered to make a covenant with them but on a condition. He was going to pluck out their right eyes as a reproach on all Israel. They asked for time to consider this ridiculous condition because offence had clouded their sense of judgement. They were vulnerable and therefore they did not carefully think the repercussions through. Never allow a Nahash into your life.

In discussing your challenging situation with 'friends', be aware that you are exposing yourself to people who may use what you tell them against you later. Your friend today is not necessarily your friend tomorrow. Remember that a man who will encourage you to be offended could be your 'killer.' Some people can rub an offence in. Avoid them, get away from the offence and move on. Offence makes you so vulnerable that you can easily sell your soul.

Sometimes, we struggle for things that God has already provided. What you are seeking today is something someone already has and does not value. What you already have is something someone else now desires. Do not despise what you have. Anytime you allow offence to control you, the enemy will capitalise on it and will take away your authority. No matter who or what you are, sometimes you will get offended so be on your guard against the wiles of the enemy. Be vigilant for the Bible tells us to be as wise as serpents but as harmless as doves. The enemy knows your area of weakness so do not expose it to him.

## Samuel's Decision

> "So Samuel said, 'Has the Lord as great delight in burnt offerings and sacrifices, As in obeying the voice of the Lord? Behold, to obey is better than sacrifice, And to heed than the fat of rams.' "
>
> 1 Samuel 15:22

In the subsequent verses, Samuel makes his position clear to Saul. A man who is rejected by God is certainly not one you should be hanging around with. Because of his loss and the possible bitterness in his heart, it is easy for the enemy to entrap you through him. Be constantly on your guard if such a person is around you. Your attention will be divided and thus you will fail to maintain your focus on God. Eventually, you would lose your effectiveness in what God wants you to do.

## Prayer

God, I bind anything that brings offence my way and destroy its potency by the reason of the anointing. I come against any devil, any hold, any plan, any trap, the means, things that contribute to offence in my life, by the reason of the anointing of the Holy Ghost, in the mighty name of Jesus. Amen.

## Reaffirm your faith with this Hymn:

My faith hath found a resting-place
Not in device nor creed
I trust the ever-living one
His wounds for me shall plead

*I need no other argument*
*I need no other plea*
*It is enough that Jesus died*
*And that He died for me.*

Leave behind anything that offends you and destroys your confidence. Even as a church, we have to leave certain things and some individuals behind. Just learn to move on. Be cheerful to adopt a positive attitude for yourself. It is said that when a man is not happy, it can shut down his system. When you are happy things go well. Create an atmosphere of joy for yourself. Do not expect joy from people or they will 'kill' you.

Jesus is aware of our weaknesses and that is why He never relied totally on man or trusted him but, looked up to God the Father. No wonder he told Peter that the cock would not crow three times before he betrayed Him. When you have the chance to help somebody, do it, as every one of us is a product of somebody's kindness. There is even a proverb that goes, "One good turn deserves another." However, for the good deeds you do, do not expect anything in return as you may never get any.

Any help you render today will be a blessing to somebody and will bring you rewards in future. It is a seed you are sowing. Galatians 6:9-10, "*And let us not grow weary while doing good, for in due season we shall reap if we do not lose heart. Therefore, as we have opportunity, let us do good to all, especially to those who belong to our family in the faith.*" Ecclesiastic 11:1 says, "*Cast your bread upon the waters, for you will find it after many days.*" Don't expect an immediate return or payback for the good you do. As happened in Luke 17: 11-19, nine of the lepers may be ungrateful and leave, but, one day one leper will come back with a heart of gratitude.

*MY PRAYER:*

*May the Lord give you glory*
*May the Lord give you favour*
*May the Lord promote you*
*May your system be strengthened*
*May God be on your side*
*May God release you in Jesus name*
*May God bless you in Jesus name. Amen.*

Chapter
# 8

# WRECKED FELLOWSHIP

Jesus revealed the nature of our hearts in Matthew 15:19. He said that out of our hearts come evil thoughts, slander, theft and false testimony. These traits can take root in us if we do not correct them. They become the very things that lead to the offensive or inappropriate behaviour that we most frequently display to our dear ones, friends, neighbours and church members etc. Paul mentions these weaknesses again in Romans 1:29-31, as wickedness, greed and depravity, envy, strife, deceit, evil mindedness, insolence, arrogance, boasting, heartlessness, disobedience and the list goes on.

Human weaknesses do not only generate offence and affect relationships, they also wreck our fellowship and that is why God abhors them. Proverbs 6:16-19, *"These six things the Lord hates, Yes seven are an abomination to Him, a proud look, a lying tongue, hands that shed innocent blood, a heart that devices wicked plans, feet that are swift in running to evil, a false witness who speaks lies, **and one who sows discord among brethren."***

Many things can cause offence in the church and make you leave the fellowship. It could be that an elder or the pastor there has hurt you; you may have suffered an injustice in the church; somebody may have been unjust to you or even looked at you with disdain. Maybe you did not get your preferred seat or someone spoke to you in a disrespectful manner and you took offence. You fall out with people and leave the fellowship vowing never to set foot there again. Or you may be unable to resolve the issues and yet still remain in the fellowship.

The enemy now knows your weakness. He knows how he can use another person to make you offended so that you decide to withdraw from the fellowship and choose instead to worship God by yourself without fellowshipping with other believers. As time goes on, you slack in your worship and gradually backslide giving the devil cause to be overjoyed. Alternatively, you move to another church. If instead of confronting and dealing with the issue, you take this course of action, you will end up hopping from church to church because of offence. You will end up becoming a 'church tourist'. You may lose your anointing because you are not settled or rooted in one place. A tree that is uprooted and replanted every few months cannot establish roots strong enough to bear fruit.

It is important to receive training under **one** spiritual authority. If you have difficulty disciplining yourself to stay under the spiritual authority of your pastor, you may find it difficult to stay under God's spiritual authority. What you are really doing is telling God in effect that you can not remain standing through tough times. How then can God use you to shepherd or counsel others? He needs strong people who will stand through the rolling of the billows and storms. He needs people who have sat **and** passed the examinations.

The other point is that if we ourselves have not learnt to submit to the authority of our leaders, why should others submit to us when we are in positions of authority? Some people choose to watch and listen to Christian television and radio, instead of going to church. My advice to you is that the Christian channel is no substitute for church.

Lack of fellowship or association with other believers suggests that you have no love and so you worship in isolation, a sure bait of the enemy. There will be no one around you to encourage you or debate things with. Ecclesiastes 4:9-10 tells us that two are better than one and that if one falls, the other will lift him up but if he is alone, there won't be anyone to help him up. The enemy can easily implant wrong ideas in your mind during such times and with no one handy to talk to you and help you dismiss them, you'll begin to draw away from God.

Ecclesiastes 4: 12, *"...a threefold cord is not quickly broken."*

It is part of the enemy's deception to tell you that you can walk with God without being part of a fellowship group. The Bible tells us to fellowship with one another and so by refusing to do so, we are trying to be independent and disobedient to God, which is sin. We need to walk in obedience for the anointing in our lives to flow both inwards and outwards. When we give out, we need to be replenished and we cannot receive if sin is a blockage.

Hebrews 10:25 *"not forsaking the assembling of ourselves together as is the manner of some is but exhorting one another"* expressed in another way, it says *"You should not stay away from the church meetings, as some are doing, but you should meet together and encourage each other."*

1 John 1:7, *"But if we live in the light, as God is in the light, we can share fellowship with each other. Then the blood of Jesus, God's Son cleanses us from every sin."*

Sometimes God places you in a fellowship for his own intentions. He may allow all kinds of unpleasant things to happen to you to strengthen you and to help your spiritual growth. That very place of opposition or hardship is what God is going to use as a springboard to promote you. Remember Joseph's experience in prison. Leaving fellowship because of offence and against the will of God is an act of disobedience. If God intended to use the situation as a test or training ground for your promotion and you leave, you have failed, lost your chance and diverted your own life or destiny from the course that God had set it on. You would also have lost the virtues or blessings that would have come to you.

### Have you passed the Test yet?

Many believers have either backslidden or left the church today, because of offence. When we are offended, unless we deal with it in the light of who we are in Christ and the word, we fall into the trap of Satan. Offence causes love to grow cold and so affects relationships. Many people today, who used to be in harmonious relationships with others, have seen them broken, destroyed or shattered and have gone their separate ways. Offence leads to hatred and betrayal and therefore has destructive consequences. It takes the grace of God to bring healing and restoration.

Some people even get offended when others are doing God's work. There is plotting, intimidation and disagreement even in the church. People bicker or argue over petty issues such as singing of musical solos, sitting positions or arrangement of flowers in the church. Issues as trivial as that can cause confusion and offence to the extent that people leave the church. Sometimes, the affected people do not leave quietly but, stir up an atmosphere of resentment, anger, hatred, revenge etc. Nehemiah was a man of God and a governor who met huge opposition from Sanballat, Tobiah, Geshem and others when he decided to go and rebuild the wall in Jerusalem. This was despite the fact that it was a project approved by God. The people were angry, ridiculed Nehemiah and tried to hinder his effort but, he was not distracted and neither did he budge nor respond with any kind of offensive behaviour in retaliation. He rather turned to God for help. They plotted to kill him, but that failed because the hand of God was on him (Nehemiah 2:19 & 20, Ch.4, Ch.6)

There is bound to be friction and arguments among people drawn from all walks of life, and they usually breed anger, frustration, unhappiness, confusion etc. Even the disciples of Jesus could not avoid disagreements as they struggled amongst themselves for positions and recognition (Luke 9:46-48). Some people seek positions in the church and when they are denied, they become offended and leave with bad feelings. The book of Ecclesiastes 7:20 indicates that, there is not a single person in all the earth who is always good and never sins. With this in mind, we should be quick to forgive. We read also in 1 John 1: 8-10: that *"If we say that we have no sin, we deceive ourselves and the truth is not in us."*

However, there will always be troublemakers who stir up strife in the home, work place, the church and the community. These are people who are victims of offence and so are likely to hurt others without realising it. We will always have amongst us in life, attention seekers, rumour mongers and complainers. You cannot please everybody in life, or keep people happy all the time, because some people will never like or agree with you whatever you do or say. Even if you are doing God's work, people may take offence as in the case of Nehemiah.

Moses had to deal with the grumblers and rebels among his own camp of Israelites in the wilderness (Numbers 11, 14 & 16). He was pushed to his limit by their criticisms, murmurings and complaints and reacted in great anger. He referred to them as rebels. He found their behaviour a burden too hard for him to bear as a leader. However, he did not pray self-centred or hateful prayers over them. Moses **prayed intercessory prayers** on behalf of the people as he cried out to God. *"I am not able to bear all these people alone, because* **the burden is too heavy for me...**" (Numbers 11:14-15). God answered his prayer and directed him to choose seventy elders who received God's spirit under his anointing to help him bear the responsibility for the people.

*If you have been hurt, the words of this Song will lift you up:*

*For you don't have to worry*
*And don't you be afraid*
*For joy comes in the morning*
*Troubles they don't last all day*
*For there is a friend in Jesus*
*He will wipe your tears away*
*If your heart is broken*
*Then lift your hands and say*

*I know that I can make it*
*I know that I can stand*
*No matter what may come my way*
*My life is in your hand*

*With Jesus I can make it*
*With him I know I can stand*
*No matter what may come my way*
*My life is in your hands*

Chapter

# 9

# THE WAY FORWARD

*"The spirit of the lord God is upon me: because the Lord hath anointed me to preach good tidings unto the meek...to bind up the broken hearted, to proclaim liberty to the captives, and the opening of the prison to them that are bound."*

Isaiah 61:1

The devil uses words spoken about you as legal ground to target his arrows at you and they become real and effective in your physical life. Words are spirit and are the basis of creation. God spoke words and they became flesh. Since He made us in His own image, whatever we utter also has the potential to create the things that we decree. This is why when curses, negative and nasty things are spoken against us they could take effect. All that the devil has to do and often does, is to act as the messenger carrying out the wishes spoken against us as soon as he has the opportunity through openings we create by our wrong lifestyles or deeds.

These become assignments to him and he takes great joy in carrying them out. This is why we have to be careful about the words we speak. When we speak ill wishes when angry and get over the anger, we may realise that we didn't really literally mean for those things to happen to the person we spoke ill against. Once bitter words are spoken, however, they have been released into the spirit realm and the devil has the legal authority to implement those words. He is roaming about like a roaring lion awaiting such opportunities and is only too quick to sei e them.

The devil uses people who talk recklessly or gossip, to speak words that bring you pain and suffering. He sends arrows to you through words. They could make you angry, upset, feel hurt, rejected, betrayed or depressed. Your feelings are hurt because of the negative criticism, your words are distorted, insults and lies are directed at you etc. Someone might intentionally try to damage your reputation.

**Even though the devil has targeted you, it is your reaction that determines whether he can carry out his assignment effectively on you or not.**

In other words, he needs your permission and cooperation in one way or the other. Jesus did not curse His opponents and neither should you. His words always gave comfort, mercy and grace and we should follow His example of forgiving and blessing. As we bless our enemies and those who mistreat us, coals of fire are heaped upon their heads (Romans 12:20).

# COUNTERACTING THE DEVIL'S STRATEGIES

## A. Refresh your Spirit

One of the most important things you need to do in order to counteract the devil's strategies is to refresh your spirit constantly by reading the Scriptures. The more you read the Scriptures and commune with God, the more He speaks to you through His spirit and the more you get to know and understand His nature and will for your life. Familiarising yourself intimately with the Scriptures develops discernment within you and enables you to be on the lookout as well as recognise the devil's strategies to offend you. Once you see through them, you can simply make up your mind to positively refuse to take offence. Laugh and tell him to 'get behind you' because you've seen what he's up to. He will cease to be effective.

## B. Let Go

Avoid holding on to offence, as it leads to many undesirable results. It takes root, grows in strength and leads to production of the fruits of offence. When a weed starts to grow and is quickly uprooted, it does not have the chance to grow into a large plant which will then entangle itself around the good plants close to it and strangle them. We are supposed to produce fruit for God's kingdom. Offended Christians cut off their own ability to produce fruits of the Spirit because their hearts are like barren ground contaminated by bitterness. Although they may still receive the gifts of the spirit, the fruits which are love, joy, peace and longsuffering, kindness, goodness, faithfulness, gentleness and self-control need to be cultivated and they require the fertile ground of our hearts. Avoid any kind of animosity, anger and bitterness.

*"Let no one become like a bitter plant that grows up and causes many troubles with its poison."*

Hebrews 12:15

## C. Love and Forgive

In Ephesians 4:31-32, Paul tells us to let all bitterness, wrath and anger, clamour, evil speaking and malice be put away from us. He tells us instead to be kind to one another, forgiving constantly and tender-hearted just as God in Christ forgave us.

Allow Jesus to intervene to heal your wounds and set you free. When Jesus told His disciples to forgive seventy times seven times, He was speaking metaphorically; meaning that no matter how many times you are offended, you should always forgive. Although this is hard, it is the Biblical antidote. Forgiveness transforms you, your life, your home and the church and fills you with peace. Forgiveness allows reconciliation and enables God's anointing and blessings to flow without hindrance into your life. Forgive those who have hurt you and your life will be refreshed and restored by Jesus.

## D. Pray and Apply the Word

The word of God, which is **the overcomer's sword and weapon**, sanctifies, shapes our minds, wills and emotions and brings healing to our souls and hearts (Psalm 19:7-15; Psalm 119:105).

Jesus prayed to God, *"sanctify them by the truth; your word is truth… For them I sanctify myself, that they too may be truly sanctified. I pray also for those who will believe…May they be brought to complete unity…"* John 17-23.

Prayer changes things and allows us to receive God's wisdom and guidance in dealing with all things including offences, hurt, and their effects.

**The areas of our lives that we especially need to guard carefully are our hearts, minds and tongues. Our sentiments, thoughts and words determine the nature of our relationships with others and this makes a big difference in our lives.**

### E. Keep Your Heart Healthy

Keep and guard your heart with all vigilance, for out of it flows the springs of life. Guard your heart so that you are not vulnerable and do not fall into the enemy's trap. Your physical heart is the source of life to the rest of your body so your whole body will be healthy if your heart pumps effortlessly without any unnecessary stress. Unnatural stress causes disease in the heart and this in turn triggers off a chain of malfunctions in the body's other organs. Get rid of all the negative emotions from your heart by forgiving the injustice, hurt, pain or whatever offence is stored up inside your heart. Lay everything at the foot of the Cross. The power of God brings healing, reconciliation and a sense of unexplainable peace deep within you. Pray for the Holy Spirit to give you the grace to be able to release the person who has offended you and caused you so much pain. As you do that, *"out of your belly shall flow rivers of living water"* (John 7:38).

Put your trust in God's righteousness so that you will enjoy His protection, kindness and favour. Psalm 36:6-10: *"Your righteousness is like the great mountains...how excellent is Your loving kindness, O God! Therefore the children of men put their trust under the shadow of Your wings. They shall be abundantly satisfied with the fatness of Your house; You shall make them drink from the river of Your pleasures, for with You is the fountain of life: in Your light shall we see light."*

Proverbs 15:13, tells us that *"A glad heart makes a cheerful countenance, but by sorrow of heart the spirit is broken."*

In Ezekiel, 36:26, God said, *"I will give you a new heart and a new mind. I will take away your stubborn heart of stone and give you an obedient heart."*

Meditate and refresh your spirit daily by reading Psalms like 139:23-24 which says *"Search me, O God, and know my heart! Try me and know my thoughts! And see if there be any wicked way in me, and lead me in the way everlasting!"* As we meditate on these words, we will be prompted to examine our hearts, take a deeper look at what is in our hearts daily so that we deal with the sin in our heart. God speaks to our hearts.

## F.   Guard Your Mind

Build a hedge around your mind, because the enemy always seeks to infiltrate it. Just as a gap in a hedge around a property allows undesirable people, things and animals to crawl into the house, so also does the enemy gain entry if we do not fortify our minds through right thinking and living. The enemy will try to push through into our minds, wrong thoughts about people, things and situations. We must measure all thoughts that flip through our minds against Biblical principles and ask ourselves whether they are in line with them before accepting them. We should also ask ourselves what our Master Jesus would have done and having determined that, do accordingly.

We should reject the wrong thoughts. You should rebuke Satan out aloud saying:

*Satan I know it's you and that is wrong. Get thee behind me.*
*I flush out these thoughts that come from you with the blood of Jesus.*
*I remind you that you are a defeated foe. I refuse to be recruited into your*
*camp. In Jesus' name. Amen.*

1 Peter 5:8 warns us to be vigilant because our adversary the devil is going about like a roaring lion seeking people to devour. We must examine our every thought, idea and motive because it could lead us to eternal life or even physical death. Your mind can be the false witness that the enemy will use to instigate offence to ensnare you. If you allow the enemy to control your thoughts and thought patterns, he gains control over you. You open up your mind to offensive thoughts and these thoughts become reality and affect your behaviour and attitude. Some Christians will go out to attack another innocent brother or sister or their spouse purely because of imagined beliefs.

Another source of erroneous thinking that leads to offence is differences in cultural backgrounds. Our perception of an issue based on our cultural or family background may differ from that of another person. We should therefore be careful not to jump to conclusions about the intents and meanings of what people say and do. We must interpret their actions and words with caution so that we are not unnecessarily offended. We also need to recognise that superstition and fear - due to cultural background - may play a part in behaviour and attitudes and we must therefore ensure that we take these into consideration when we interpret issues. It is also important to ensure that our own erroneous cultural beliefs do not conflict with our Christian faith. At all times, we should try to line our thoughts with the word of God, because it is a revelation of truth and that will sanctify our minds and will radically transform us.

Romans 12:2 cautions us not to be conformed to this world and become adapted to its external superficial customs and ways but, rather to be transformed and changed by the entire renewal of our minds. This can be done through developing new ideas and attitudes that are in line with Jesus' teaching. Furthermore, Paul in 2 Corinthians 5:17 tells us that if any man is in Christ he is an entirely new creation. The old and previous moral and spiritual condition has passed away and the fresh and new has come.

## G. Mind Your Tongue

*"And if anyone does not offend in speech, he is a fully developed character and a perfect man able to control his whole body and to curb his entire nature."*

James 3:2

James is telling us that if we can take control over our tongues, we can not only consider ourselves fully developed in godly character but, we will also be in control of our bodies and our nature. *"Let every man be swift to hear, slow to speak, slow to wrath..."* (James 1:19-20).

Watch your words carefully, so that when you are offended, you do not sin with your mouth. Although the tongue is a very small part of the body, it has very great power. Just as a tiny spark can set a whole forest ablaze, so also can the tongue cause great confusion and trouble. The tongue is not easily tamed and is full of deadly poison in the natural. The same tongue that is used to give thanks to God is sadly also used to curse others. We are tempted to lash out with our tongues when offended. We may become confrontational, use unbefitting language or get so angry that we say things that cause us to lose respect and grace. At the very least we regret our words when we calm down.

A bad reputation is not like a bit of mud that can be easily washed off. A person's reputation once soiled is not easily restored. It takes just a moment to destroy but a lifetime to build. One's behaviour leaves an almost indelible impression on the mind. If you have a good reputation and command authority, an irrational act or emotional over-reaction can completely destroy that reputation and the respect you command.

Meditating on these wise sayings should be a useful guide:

Proverbs 18:7, *"A fool's mouth is his ruin, and his lips are a snare to himself."*

Proverbs 18:21 *"Death and life are in the power of the tongue, and those who love it will eat its fruits."*
Proverbs 15:28 *"The mind of the righteous ponders how to answer, but*

*the mouth of the wicked pours out evil things."*

Ecclesiastic 10:12-13 *"What the wise say brings them honour, but fools are destroyed by their own words. They start out with silly talk and end up with pure madness."* (Good News Bible.)

Colossians 4:6 *"Let your speech at all times be gracious (pleasant and winsome), seasoned (as it were) with salt, so that you may never be at a loss to know how to answer anyone who puts a question to you."* (Amplified version)

Refresh your spirit daily with: Psalm 19:14 which says, *"Let the words of my mouth and the meditation of my heart be acceptable in Your sight O Lord my strength and my redeemer."*

Psalm 141:3 *"Set a guard over my mouth, O Lord, keep watch over the door of my lips."*

Proverbs 4:24 also tells us to put away from ourselves *"false and dishonest speech, and wilful and contrary talk"*.

## H. Seek Help

Luke 17:1, Jesus said … *"Woe unto him through whom offence come."* We all do offend but if you are the one who always sows seeds of discord then:
- Be honest about it and deal with it. Admit your mistakes.
- Learn to say sorry.
- Repent and pray for the blood of Jesus to cleanse you.
- If your temper stirs up quickly when you are offended, or if it causes you to offend then you may want to consider it as a yoke that needs breaking through the anointing or power

of God.

o Remind yourself: *"He who is slow to anger has great understanding, but he who has a hasty temper exalts folly."* Proverbs 14:29

o Proverbs 15:18 *"A hot-tempered man stirs up strife, but he who is slow to anger quiets contention."*

Seek practical help such as counselling, anger management, communication skills and other appropriate solutions for your situation.

## I.   Forgive the Offender and Forget the Offence

Forgiveness brings transformation and reconciliation and enables God's blessings to flow into your life.

The following story is the wonderful testimony of Sister Angela. It clearly shows how if we can humbly let go of pride and forgive, God restores and prospers us. There was this lady called Angela in my congregation whose marriage had broken down. For a number of years she had lived on her own supporting their children who lived with relatives in Ghana. Life was a real struggle. Then she met another man, fell in love and they had a lavish, beautiful wedding in the church. They seemed to be getting on well. There was no hint of any problems. About a year later, without any warning, her husband got up early one morning and walked out saying that he felt that the marriage wasn't working. She was perplexed at this strange turn of events and tried to get him to talk but, he wouldn't and left. She was devastated and confused. She did a lot of soul searching but could find no reason for it.

Prior to his leaving, she had booked a flight to visit her children so she went. On her return she found that her husband had returned to the apartment and cleared out everything and gone. There was not even a spoon left. Even the carpets were gone. As she couldn't financially afford to replace the basic essentials at that point in time, she went to live with a friend. She spent time praying and seeking God's face as to what was happening to her life.

According to her, the Lord started to impress upon her spirit that she should contact her first husband. He lived in France and she had not had any contact with him in years. She struggled against what the Lord was telling her because it did not make sense to her. They had divorced and she had remarried since then - even though her new husband had disappeared. She did not even have the address of her first husband. The Lord gave her no peace. Eventually she found out his phone number through contacts. She phoned him not knowing what to say and was surprised by his friendly response. At the Lord's prompting, she humbly asked him to forgive her for the things she'd done, putting aside all pride. They talked and he invited her to visit him.

She went and they talked. She told him about her re-marriage and life since they parted. He told her that he had not remarried because his heart was still hers. They renewed their friendship and on her return he gave her money to buy all that she needed to go back to her apartment. She was able to furnish her home like a home fit for a queen. In addition to that he gave her funds to start a business. He also asked her to remarry him. She agreed and got her divorce and they had a new wedding. Today, they are very happily remarried and prospering greatly. Angela's testimony was that once she had forgiven her then ex husband, listened to God, overcome pride and apologised, God started blessing her.

God had obviously moved the wrong husband out of her life so that she could go back to the one God always intended for her.

The first marriage was the one that God had sanctioned for her but, she made a wrong choice and her life was off course until she went back to her first husband. God then began to open doors for her and bless her. She succeeded in many areas where she had previously failed - including business, finance, obtaining visas for her children to join her, a new big house and favour where she did not expect it. She felt so overwhelmed by the blessings and favour that God was pouring on her within the period just after she obeyed God and apologised, that she was often overwhelmed with tears. She said the abundance of blessings was so great that she didn't know if she could bear to receive any more. God has continued to bless her and the family mightily.

Angela's testimony shows the results of obedience to God and illustrates how we block our own blessings through unforgiving attitudes, pride and holding onto offence in our hearts. Releasing people through forgiveness opens the doors to our blessings. All those blessings were waiting for Angela. Had she known, she would not have left her first marriage and would not have suffered those years of hardship and unhappiness. Had she also not listened and been obedient to God and taken the path of reconciliation, she would have missed out on all that the Lord had in store for her. She passed the test and is reaping the benefits.

Has the Lord set you a test? Are you bearing a grudge? Are you too proud to say sorry? Are you holding bitterness in your heart? Have you got the guts to let it go and open the door to receive your blessings like Angela?

Avoid any kind of animosity, anger, bitterness as much as possible, and do not focus on the offence. Ephesians 4:31-32 *"get rid of all bitterness, passion and anger..."*

Colossians 3:12-13 *"...but now put them all away: anger, wrath, malice, slander, and foul talk from your mouth. Do not lie to one another...and if one has a complaint against another, forgive each other, as the Lord has forgiven you, so you must also forgive..."*

The Lord's prayer says, *"forgive us our trespasses as we forgive those that trespass against us."* Jesus also tells us, *"If ye forgive men their trespasses, your heavenly father will also forgive you"* (Matthew 6:12,14).

## J. Confess the sin in your heart to God and repent for his forgiveness

Isaiah 1:18, *"Come now, and let us reason together, says the Lord: though your sins be as scarlet, they shall be as white as snow: though they be red as crimson; they shall be as wool."*

Verbalise the offence to somebody you trust to be compassionate, or who identifies with you, to gain your freedom. Do not repress your feelings. Proverbs 28: 13; 1 John 1: 9

Where the offence has made life more difficult for you, forgive by faith, for such forgiveness is an act of obedience to God. Let go of the pain, hurt, sadness, self-pity and move on. You are not the only one who has ever been offended. Even in the most perfect conditions we will still be offending each other. When it is over and dealt with choose not to bring it up or talk about it anymore. When a painful memory of it comes into your thoughts, dismiss it. It is the enemy trying to take you back into its bondage again. Sing hymns and praises instead and they will push the thoughts out of your mind. The peace and the joy of worshiping God will replace the negative thoughts. The pain and sadness will also shrink into insignificance as you sing praise and glorify God.

## K. Reconciliation

> *"Therefore if you bring your gift to the altar, and there remember that your brother has something against you, leave your gift there before the altar, and go your way, first to be reconciled to your brother, and then come and offer your gift."*
> Matthew 5:23-24

Here Jesus is telling us that we must make it our top priority to reconcile with our brethren. It is so important that it must be done before we make our offering to the Lord. Furthermore our offering will not be acceptable to the Almighty if we do not first reconcile with those who hold anything against us. It does not matter who is at fault or caused the offence. If it is the other person, by seeking reconciliation, we help him to come out of offence and the consequences of holding onto offence which might otherwise lead him to hell.

In seeking reconciliation, we might even find that the offence was caused through inaccurate information being passed or received, misinterpretation of information, distortion, or wrong discernment of our motives.

To reconcile takes humility and that requires maturity. We must be willing to humble ourselves and apologise, meaning it from deep within our hearts, to the offended party.

God loves both Christians and non-Christians, good and bad people. Jesus challenges us to love those who work against us to destroy us as we emulate His character. On the cross, He prayed to God to forgive even those who were killing Him. Any of us would have been inclined to curse them with the worst imaginable curses, calling for brimstone and fire to be heaped on their heads and all their future generations. In Matthew 5: 38-48, Jesus tells us how we should relate to our enemies. In verses 44 and 45 he says *"But I say to you, love your enemies and pray for those who persecute you, so that you may be sons of your Father who is in Heaven for he makes his sun rise on the evil and the good"*

He gave His life willingly to reconcile us back to God our Father. Nobody else is better qualified to teach us about reconciliation. We cannot carry out any reconciliation without love.

We therefore have to ask God to help us through His spirit and grace to develop love for our enemies so that we can effectively and genuinely pray for them as this releases us into our blessings, anointing and destinies. Paul in 2 Corinthians 2: 5-11 says that when a brother has hurt or offended even the entire church and who in turn have united to punish him, the church must after that, forgive and comfort him, showing him renewed love so that he will not become so discouraged that he won't be able to recover. As you forgive him your father in heaven forgives you also.

Paul writes in Romans 12:17-19 to *"**Live in harmony** with one another…Repay no one evil for evil… if possible, so far as it depends on you live peaceably with all. Never avenge yourselves, but leave it to the wrath of God."* He goes on to advice us in Ephesians 5:1-2 to *"**be imitators of God** as dear children and walk in love, as Christ also has* *loved us and given Himself for us, an offering and a sacrifice to God for a sweet-smelling aroma."* We must therefore support one another spiritually and emotionally.

*"If your enemy is hungry, give him bread to eat; and if he is thirsty, give him water to drink; for you will heap coals of fire on his head and the Lord will reward you"* (Romans 12:20).

If you are in a position to help your enemy, do so **out of love**, and God will surely bless you. Your motives in helping him must be pure not with the intention of heaping the coals on his head. It is only in so doing that God will punish him and reward you.

This is not an easy advice to take. You might say that *"you do not know what they did to me."* Jesus Christ did not say it would be easy to forgive and release them from their debt of pain. It may be true that you feel that you should pay them back and that you can't stand to see them get away with their acts but this is where we are tested as Christians. If we judge and take revenge, we are setting ourselves up as judges and God will judge us according to the same standards that we judge others. This is dangerous for us because we are so imperfect and so sinful. If it were not for the grace of God, where would we be? Psalm 130:3 says *"If You, Lord should keep account of and mark our iniquities, O Lord, who can stand?"*

## L.  Restoration

When we handle offence in the way prescribed in the scriptures by our Redeemer and King we are restored. Through the scriptures we learn from the mistakes of those who did not handle offence correctly and suffered various consequences. This includes people like the servant in Matthew 18:25-27, who owed his master a debt and could not pay. The master decided to forgive him the total debt and write it off. He however, went away and had his fellow servant thrown into jail for a smaller debt owed to him. When his master heard this, he changed his mind and had him, his wife and children sold to pay the debt. When you act with a pure heart, exercise forgiveness and don't take matters into your own hands, God blesses you.

Remember the story of the prodigal son who asked for his share of his father's inheritance before time. He squandered all the money, regretted it, repented and asked for forgiveness. His father could have refused to forgive him but he forgave him and there was partying and rejoicing, reconciliation and restoration of the relationship (Luke 15:11-22). This is in parallel with God our Father accepting Jesus' atonement for our sins and reconciling us back to himself and restoring us back to his loving arms. It also reflects how there is rejoicing in heaven when one sinner repents.

Chapter

# 10

# CONCLUSION

*Summary of effects of offence;*
o   It can make you curse God
o   You cannot flow in the anointing
o   It can distract and divert you from the destiny God has planned for you
o   It is the trap of the enemy to stop what God has purposed for you in life
o   You could die a foolish death
o   You will forget your manners and lose control
o   It will keep you away from the glory of God
o   It will take away your promotion
o   It can cause you to be vindictive
o   It can cause sickness
o   It will make you lose your authority
o   It can frustrate you, kill your vision and dreams
o   It limits you
o   You cannot focus or concentrate on what you should do
o   It will break you down physically, emotionally, psychologically and spiritually
o   It will make you unnecessarily confrontational
o   It will dampen your spirit and depress you
o   You will not be able to receive from God

- o   You can lose your position due to your reactions to offence
- o   It perpetrates violence and can lead to commitment of a criminal act in the eyes of the law
- o   It can make you arrogant
- o   It can make you forget what God has promised you
- o   It can destroy your faith
- o   It can distract and divert your attention from what God wants you to see or do
- o   It can cause you to be replaced by wrong people
- o   It can steal your joy
- o   It will make you lose the correct strategies of battle
- o   It will make you lose what you have laboured for
- o   It can take away your protective mechanism
- o   It can destroy homes and create division in families
- o   It causes you to lose your dignity
- o   It can take away your privileges and then you will associate yourself with worthless characters who will be of a hindrance to you......and many more!

Offences vary and are numerous and must be dealt with biblically so that we do not lose our right standing with God. If we lose this we would not only fail to fulfil our destinies but also fail to make it to heaven and eternal life with God.

**DEALING WITH OFFENCE:**

Examples of how to deal with offence sensibly and find solution through forgiveness in a way prescribed by God:

**A.   Forgiveness**

There are two basic steps.

### A1.  Where we have offended someone

Matthew 5:23-24 *"Therefore if you bring your gift to the altar, and there remember that your brother has something against you, leave your gift there before the altar, and go your way, first to be reconciled to your brother, and then come and offer your gift."*

It is important that you take the initiative to approach the offended party with the right attitude if you really want to seek reconciliation. You need to go with an attitude of humility rather than pride. Pride and seeking to justify yourself will only fuel the flames and make matters worse. Going to seek reconciliation and saying to the offended party, "I'm sorry but you were partly to blame because you ......" or "you just don't understand me" only means you are still holding on to pride in your heart and this can never bring true peace. Listen and hold your tongue till they have finished talking. If you disagree, let the person know that you respect their views and let them know that you will search your attitude and intentions. Then tell them that you are sorry that you have hurt them. If however you realise that their assessment of you is correct, just humbly tell them, "You are right. I am sorry. Please forgive me." Having done this, you have been wise. Godly wisdom is willing to yield.

### A2.  Where we have been offended

Temptation to take action to get even may be great but, through the power of the Holy Spirit in us, we can overcome it as King David showed us in 1 Samuel 26: 9-11. King Saul was making every effort to seek out David and kill him. David who had done nothing wrong against Saul had to flee and was in hiding sleeping in caves and the wilderness. At one point whilst Saul's army was pursuing David, God put Saul's army of 3000 soldiers into deep sleep and David with Abishai were able to sneak into their camp right through to where Saul was sleeping. Abishai pleaded with David to allow him to kill Saul with a spear, saying that the Lord had delivered his enemy into his hand and that had their positions been reversed, Saul would have not hesitated to kill him.

All the reasons sounded good and made sense and David would have felt totally justified to let Abishai put a spear through Saul <u>BUT</u> he said, "*Do not destroy him; for who can stretch out his hand against the Lord's anointed, and be guiltless.*" David would not avenge himself and left it in the hands of the Lord. It is no wonder that God refers to David as a man after His own heart. David in spite of his mistakes was always obedient and repentant. How many of us would have had a heart like David's? How many of us would have resisted the pressure and wrong counsel of friends, especially when what they are advising seems to make such sense?

We aim to win our brother who has offended us so we must be willing to forgive him and to restore the relationship. Even though we generally no longer kill with physical swords, we destroy, crush and ruin each other with a sword of another kind, the tongue. Proverbs 18:21 says death and life are in the power of the tongue. Use your words to compliment and encourage people instead of putting them down.

Jesus emphasises the importance of forgiveness. In Matthew 6:14-15 Jesus says, "*For if you forgive people their trespasses, your heavenly Father will also forgive you. But if you do not forgive others their trespasses, neither will your Father forgive you your trespasses."* When Jesus says something He means every word of it. Quite often we say to others and even tell ourselves that we have forgiven. If God searches our hearts will He find true forgiveness?

Let us seriously consider:-
  o  How many Christians would want God to forgive them in the same way they have forgiven those who have offended them. The way we forgive and release another person is the same way we will be forgiven.
  o  Would you rather be convicted by the Holy Spirit now and experience genuine repentance and forgiveness? Or would you rather hold onto your pride and your legal rights and refuse to forgive and hear the master say, "Depart"?

The love of Jesus for us transcends all we could ever do. If He'd had to wait for us to come to Him and apologise, saying "We were wrong. You were right. Forgive us", He would still be waiting. We would have had no forgiveness from the cross.

## B. Repent

What leads men to repentance? In Romans 2:4, we read that God's goodness and kindness is at the root of repentance. His love does not leave us condemned to hell. He proved his love by sending Jesus, His only son to die on the cross for us. God reaches out first, even though we have sinned against Him. He reaches out not to condemn but to restore and to save.

Since we are to imitate God, we are to extend reconciliation to a brother who sins against us. Matthew 18:15 says *"Moreover if your brother sins against you, go and tell him his fault between you and him alone. If he hears you, you have gained your brother."*

Many people apply this scripture with a different attitude from what Jesus taught us. They confront the offender in a spirit of revenge and anger and use the verse as justification to condemn the one who has hurt them. Jesus instructed us to go to one another not for condemnation but for reconciliation, not to tell our brother how they have offended us. We are to go **to remove the breach** preventing the restoration of our relationship. The Lord Himself promises us restoration when we come to Him with a repentant heart, *"therefore also now, saith the Lord, turn ye even to me with all your heart..."* (Joel 2.).

## C. Show True Love and Reconcile

We need to ask ourselves, whether we are willing to kill our pride in order to be reconciled with the one who has offended us. As we ask ourselves this we must remember that out of love God reached out to us before we asked for forgiveness. Love never fails and it shall cover the multitude of sins (1 Peter 4:8).

Jesus said *"Blessed are the peacemakers for they shall be called the sons of God"* (Matthew 5:9). Please note that He did not say, Blessed are the 'peacekeepers'. A peacekeeper does everything including compromising truth to keep peace. This however results only in an artificial, touchy and superficial peace that often does not last. A peacemaker will go in love and confront issues, bringing truth so that the resulting reconciliation will be a lasting one. He desires openness, truth and love. He refuses to hide offence with a politically correct smile. At the end what a peacemaker achieves is a bond of love that no evil can sever. Remember, **the bottom line is love**.

If we love we will forgive and we will also pray meaningfully for our enemies and those who offend us. If we can pray for them asking God to meet them at their point of need and for them to be blessed from the depths of our hearts and souls, then we know we have truly forgiven them.

I pray that the Holy Spirit will give us the strength to examine our hearts and truly release those who we are holding grudges against, so that we are able to remain in the will of God. Colossians 3: 12-13 says that *"...as the elect of God, holy and beloved, put on tender mercies, kindness, humility, meekness, long suffering: bearing with one another, and forgiving one another, if any one has a complaint against another; even as Christ forgave you so you also must do."*

If we do not forgive, we will not have any real peace in our hearts. A person who cannot forgive has forgotten how great a debt God has forgiven them.

Romans 5:8-10, *"But God demonstrates His own love towards us, in that while we were still sinners, Christ died for us...For if, when we were enemies, we were reconciled to God through the death of His Son, much more having been reconciled, we shall be saved by His life."*

## D. Intercede For The Offender.

Jesus said in Matthew 5:43-45, to love, bless and do good to our enemies and pray for those who persecute us. Job had a loving heart and never cursed God in his afflictions. He rejected the wrong counsel of his wife and friends to curse God, but instead became an intercessor for them. *"And the Lord restored the fortunes of Job, when he had prayed for his friends; and the Lord gave Job twice as much as he had before"* (Job 42:10).

## REWARDS FOR OBEDIENCE

### A. Your Reward

Romans 13 tells us that God will judge and reward us according to our obedience to his commands; how we treat people, including our response to His command to forgive those who offend us, how we relate to our brothers and sisters even those in authority civil or church. David wrote *"Blessed is he whose transgression is forgiven whose sin is covered. Blessed is the man unto whom the Lord imputeth not iniquity, and in whose spirit there is no guile"* Psalm 32:1-2.

### B. The Assurance of Victory

Be a person of integrity, be Christ-like, live in His Spirit even when you are offended. Feed yourself on His word daily and act on it and it will give you revelation for your healing. It will sanctify you and set you free and you will be triumphant, stronger and able to handle other offences when they come. Encourage yourself with Job's words in Job 23:12. *"He hath*

*esteemed the words of His mouth more than my necessary food."*
Romans 8:37 says "Know that in all these things offence, trials,
distress, persecution, hurt, pain etc. we are more than conquerors
through Him who loved us."

Revelations 12:11 says, we are overcomers and we overcome
Satan by the blood of the Lamb and the words of our testimony,
as he is the one that instigates offence in the first place. Remind
yourself that offence is the trap of Satan.

## ROLE OF THE CHURCH

The church should be a place where people do not offend one
another causing some to stumble. It must be a place with an
atmosphere of love, comfort, restoration and the building up of
one another. Only then will there be peace and unity with the
anointing of God flowing like a stream. This will then lead to
miracles and healings as in the Acts of the Apostles; for where
God finds unity, He commands blessings. It is only when this is
happening that the body of Christ can impact society
significantly. The rivalry and divisions within the church today
have riddled the body with holes and are affecting the move of
God. Remember that you are the salt of the earth and must not
lose your flavour.

**Sing these Songs Unto the Lord:**

1. *Oh master Jesus*
2. *We give you praise*
3. *We give you glory*
4. *You are the Son of God*

**Song**

*There is none Holy as the Lord*
*There is none besides him*
*Neither is there any rock like our God*
*There is none Holy as the Lord*

**Songs**

1. Oh Lord my God
2. Blessed assurance
3. Great is thy faithfulness
4. On a hill far away
5. Hallelujah, hallelujah
6. There is none Holy as the Lord
7. God is so good.
8. 'tis so sweet to trust in Jesus
9. I am trusting thee Lord Jesus
10. Holy, Holy, Holy
11. mercy rewrote my life

**FINAL WORDS**

I hope and believe that God has used this book to refresh you and bring healing to your wounds and enabled you to let go of all offences and seek reconciliation with those you need to, so that you can be restored to your rightful place in life. Do not let offence or anybody hold you down or cause you to stumble. Do not hold on to any grudges. Remind yourself that at the name of Jesus every knee shall bow and every tongue shall confess that Jesus is Lord.

**God bless you.**

## How to Receive Jesus Christ as Lord and Saviour in Your Life

**I John 1:9** says that, 'If we confess our sins, he is faithful and just to forgive us our sins, and to cleanse us from all unrighteousness.' Jesus loves you regardless of who you **are** and what you have done.

**Romans 10:9-10** also says that, 'If thou shalt confess with thou mouth the Lord Jesus, and shalt believe in thine heart that God hath raised him from the dead, thou shalt be saved. For with the heart man believeth unto righteousness; and with the mouth confession is made unto salvation.'

Do you want to receive Jesus as your Lord and Saviour? Are you far from the Lord and want Him to come and be Lord in every area of your life? If the answer to any of these questions is yes, then make the following confessions with me so that we can make Jesus Lord over every area of our lives. Pray from the depths of your heart. Believe it as you speak it, and you shall be saved.

Dear Jesus,

I believe that you died on the Cross for me and that you rose again on the third day. On the Cross you took away my sins, my diseases and my infirmities. You blotted out the handwriting of ordinances that were against me, which were contrary to me, with your blood and took them out of the way, nailing it to your Cross. You became a curse for me, so that I might be free.

I confess to you that I am a sinner and that I need your love and forgiveness. Come into my life today, Lord Jesus, and give me eternal life. I confess you now as my Lord. Thank you Jesus for dying for me. Thank you for my salvation.

Signed   _____

Date      _____

Write to us and we will send you information to help you with your new life in Christ.

Mailing Addresses:

**The Miracle Centre**
P. O. Box 8786
London
NW2 1WR
England

**Worldwide Miracle Outreach**
P. O. Box AN 16618
Accra-North
Ghana
West Africa

**Telephone:**    +44 (0) 207 357 0910
**Website:**      www.lawrencetetteh.org
www.miracletouch.org

**Books In Print By Dr Lawrence Tetteh**
- Count Your Blessings
- Do Miracles Still happen?
- Lord, I Need A Miracle
- Understanding Deliverance
- Rescue the Perishing
- Possessing your Possession
- Benefits of the Anointing

*For further information about Videos And Audio Tapes, write to:*

*Worldwide Miracle Outreach*
*P. O. Box 8786*
*London NW2 1WR*
*www.lawrencetetteh.org*

*Are you in need of prayer? Would you want us to agree with you in prayer?*
*Please fill the following and mail it to us at the address below:*

Name _____

           **Title**        **Print Surname first**

Address _____

City _____

Postcode _____

Tel No [Day] [Eve] _____

*Please tick the appropriate box for your prayer request.*

[ ] Health     [ ] Unemployed   [ ] Abuse     [ ] Marriage  [ ] Addiction
[ ] Deliverance  [ ] Job        [ ] Bereavement  [ ] Other.........................

Please mail this to: The Miracle Centre, P. O. Box 8786, London NW2 1WR

As
these plans
continue to unfold,
the world is witnessing the
emergence of
Dr. Lawrence Tetteh as one of
the most uncompromising and
powerful healing evangelists of
our time.

- Dr. T. L. Osborne